To an old and dear friend,
Gerald ~ the much-published —
from a first-time loser

Don

THE FACE OF MINNEAPOLIS

THE FACE OF

MINNEAPOLIS

PHOTOGRAPHY, JEROME LIEBLING   TEXT, DON MORRISON

DILLON PRESS, Inc.   Minneapolis, Minnesota   □   Cover and Title Art by DICK SUTPHEN

*T*TO BE PERFECTLY HONEST, it was only 15 years ago that I started to devote any serious attention to Minneapolis. That was when I accepted a job offer and moved here.

Before that, I had only a schoolboy awareness of the twin cities of Minneapolis-St. Paul —the hyphen was a part of the name so far as I was concerned.

There also were fuzzy connotations of stage-dialect Swedes, flour mills and something about iron mines.

Minneapolis, to sever the umbilical hyphen, was not a city that impinged upon my consciousness. In fact, I doubt that it impinges strongly on the national consciousness. Not 15 years ago, at any rate.

The reason, I think, is that it is not a crossroads. Almost any traveler, going anywhere, will pass through Denver, Kansas City, Baltimore, St. Louis or Atlanta.

He is unlikely to pass through Minneapolis en route to somewhere else because there is not that much else on the other side. This is not to slight the people of the Dakotas and points northwestward. They are grand people, but there just aren't very many of them. There are no major cities beyond Minneapolis until you reach Seattle or Portland on the Pacific Coast, well over a thousand miles distant.

Travel follows the paths of commerce. Heavy traffic develops between big market areas, namely population centers.

In this sense, Minneapolis is a terminus. Most travelers who come here, come here on purpose, as I did. It is a large and prosperous city and it attracts considerable commercial interchange from other large and prosperous cities to the south and east—but to them it surely must seem the end of the line.

The vast majority of Americans, having no specific reason to come here and no occasion to pass through, never will. They may be forgiven if Minneapolis does not loom large in their daily thoughts. I hope I may be forgiven my earlier indifference to the city I now think of as my own. Had anyone told me 20 years ago that I would be living in Minneapolis, I would have given him a tolerant pat on the head.

It was pure chance that I came here. I could otherwise have gone to my grave without ever laying eyes on the place. I am glad that did not happen.

We newspapermen have a vocational peculiarity. We tend to take jobs that are offered to us, either because we don't like the one we have or because we don't have one not to like.

I was living in New York when I was offered a job on the Minneapolis Tribune. The pay was impressive—sixty-five dollars a week. I felt ready, after five years of spirit-wearying Manhattan life, to live elsewhere.

But, to continue the note of candor, I had no intention of remaining here. I considered Minneapolis nothing more than a way-station on my way further West. I felt the vague call of mountains and ocean. It was my thought to put in a couple years in Swedesville, then push on to an assignation with destiny in Denver or San Francisco. After all, who wants to live in Minneapolis?

I had overlooked, however, the principle stated above. You don't pass through Minneapolis on your way to someplace else. I'm still here.

In pursuit of my policy of painful truth, I must admit that for the first two years I cordially disliked Minneapolis. There was no animosity about it, merely a lack of understanding. Possibly the contrast with New York was too wrenching. Perhaps it was because I was working nights—newspapermen frequently live on the dark side of the moon —and was tardy in discovering the town in full light. There were small irritations, too.

I was irritated, for example, with the kind of churchiness that extends into the public realm and forbade me to buy a drink on Sunday or after one a. m. (I still am, for that matter, but have come to more tolerant terms with such ingrained midwestern puritopieties).

It is correct to say that my first two years in Minneapolis were not a honeymoon. Instead, they were like a marriage of convenience, in which stranger-spouses slowly come to know one another and, with knowledge find liking —and finally love.

Imperceptibly, my wife and I spoke less and less of moving on. The loom of mountains faded on my mental retina; the sea-salt tang no longer whiffed at my imagination's nostrils. One startling day, I turned down an unsought job offer from Denver. It was comical, but the Morrisons rather shamefacedly had to admit to each other that we did not want to leave Minneapolis, despite all our big talk.

What had happened? This is the poignant question I shall be nibbling at in this book. After all, what is so special about Minneapolis?

My commitment to honesty forces me to confess that I don't really know. I will say straight out that there is nothing so terribly special about Minneapolis as it is measured against other American cities of comparable size. In one sense—looking at the coarse grain rather than the fine—it is typical to the point of banality.

It is a sad fact of our industrial society that we all become more typical with each fiscal year. Regional differences, save those of climate and of topography, blend and blur at an increasing rate. Simply as people, we laugh simultaneously, coast to coast, at a comic turn on TV; we tap our feet to the same tune echoing in every corner of the land; we instantaneously adopt catch phrases from magazines and syndicated newspaper writers; we read the best-selling books en masse and are obedient to all the changes of style.

As residents of hamlet, town, city or metropolis, we live more and more in identical settings. Our houses look alike, or rather they no longer reflect any particular locality: there are Cape Cod cottages in Little Rock and California ranch houses on Long Island. Every big airport looks like every other big airport and—with jets that fly a thousand miles in the time it takes to read a magazine —you lose the sense of getting somewhere as well as that of arriving.

Finally, our mass-producing, mass-marketing economy has created near-total uniformity in those items of daily use that make up our outward existence. It is as though the material trappings of our lives have melted and blended down into a thick fudge sauce of national brand names, labels, trademarks, emblems, slogans and standardized products which has drowned the regional flavor and color that formerly distinguished one part of the country from another.

Continent-wide, we drive the same makes of cars, open the same brand of canned beans, drink known-label booze, wear chain store clothes, squeeze the top-selling toothpaste tube and go about our business through avenues lined with signs, filling stations, store fronts and company names that are duplicated endlessly in every community around the compass.

Only a handful of American cities are truly and dramatically distinctive. New York, New Orleans, San Francisco, Washington, Boston, Miami, Charleston, Las Vegas strike the visitor immediately with their special personalities, their unique color or excitement or atmosphere or beauty or gaudy awfulness.

We can claim no such aura for Minneapolis, which does not proclaim its essential Minneapolis-ness at first glance, or second or third. It took me two years, remember, before I began to perceive the qualities that made me want to adopt it as my hometown.

Its distinctions are of the fine-grain order, most of them unassertive, but they do add up impressively: if you look closely, Minneapolis can be seen as profoundly different from its cheek-by-jowl neighbor, St. Paul, and vitally different from other cities of the Midwest and elsewhere.

To speak of distinctions implies comparisons, but that is not my purpose. Other cities (St. Paul included) can write their own books.

Communities have climates unrelated to meteorology. Each one has its own complex social, cultural, intellectual and civic climate that is the average of the attitudes and habits and energies and preferences of its inhabitants. Each has its own beauty or lack of it; each has its sufficiency or scarcity of opportunities for work, play, comfort, challenge; each is at a greater or lesser distance from other population centers and is influenced accordingly.

Assuming a person is free to choose his place of residence (and assuming he really cares where, why and how he lives) he will settle where he finds the most congenial balance of all these factors.

I live in Minneapolis by choice, not necessity. I have visited or lived in most other major cities in the United States. To me, Minneapolis is one of the most habitable. It is considered a beautiful city and it is, but it has much ugliness, also. Its winter climate is formidable indeed, but I prefer its human climate to virtually every other city of my acquaintance.

So, perhaps some final comments are in order concerning the kind of things I intend to say and why.

First off, this is not a history of Minneapolis. Neither is it an attempt at a comprehensive survey of the city's every facet and aspect. The histories already have been written and I have neither the space, the patience, the knowledge or the inclination to turn every stone in Minneapolis.

One thing this book definitely will not be: It will not be a piece of puffery, a booster's brochure, a Chamber of Commerce chapbook. If you care enough about a thing to admire it, you also should care enough to criticize its faults, of which Minneapolis has many. I happen to think its virtues outweigh the faults, but faults exist and should be acknowledged.

Obviously, liking is a personal thing and the reader is warned that whatever I shall subsequently say about Minneapolis is purely personal. These will be my own reactions, observations, perceptions, prejudices and conclusions. You will, if you continue to read, be subjected to a probable excess of subjectivity. In full first-person spate, I shall be judging Minneapolis and you will be free to judge me. So be it and good luck to us both. Merely to identify, let alone describe, the subtle, intricate, often contradictory spirit of a city is not a task you tackle head-on without the woeful risk of being dogmatic and arbitrary. Let me then be both, honestly and openly. Every one of you has his or her own feelings about our town. Many of you could express them better. None of us would be wholly right.

I have never before seriously attempted to analyze the larger and smaller elements that I have found attractive in Minneapolis.

I would rather not be serious, if you don't mind. I would rather be foolish than solemn in an assignment like this. I would rather falter in my quest than arrive at such certitude about Minneapolis that even I would know I was wrong. The man who can describe precisely why he loves a woman does not know what love is—and he certainly does not know the woman.

Spirit and personality are tenuous things. As such, they are elusive quarry to capture. I am further handicapped because I am not sure in what part of the forest my quarry hangs out. Should I happen to stumble on any worthwhile game, I am certain the surprise will be mutual.

OLE BULL, LORING PARK

VIEW OF MISSISSIPPI RIVER LOCKS, TENTH AVENUE BRIDGE

GRANITE STATUE, PIONEERS SQUARE

INDIAN POWWOW

BRONZE STATUE OF GUNNAR WENNERBERG, MINNEHAHA PARK

FROM FOSHAY TOWER, LOOKING WEST

*I*N COMMON WITH MOST CITIES of the American Midwest, Minneapolis is short on history. It is the product of diligence, of commercial opportunity, of favorable location, of generations of people going quietly and steadily about their own affairs.

There is no grand sweep of historical events to engrave upon the banners of Minneapolis. No armies have wheeled and clashed under its walls; it has neither produced nor received any conquerers; it has known nothing so historically stylish as a plague or an earthquake —in fact, it cannot even boast a good rousing fire.

Only a little more than a century ago, Minneapolis was literally a cottage small by a waterfall. From that, it simply grew by addition and multiplication. There is nothing shameful, certainly, about such tidy increase. But, there is nothing very romantic, either. In 1850, the year the first house was built in Minneapolis, a Library Association already existed in St. Anthony, the pioneer "parent" community across the river that later was absorbed by its lusty offspring. By 1851, a Masonic lodge had been organized. Hardly the stuff of epic poems.

Romance of the storybook variety had departed the area long before the industrious settlers arrived with hammer and saw and ledger to found today's industrious, middle-class city.

But, what romance there was was robust 17th century romance: Tiny bands of French missionaries and fur-traders feeling their way into the wilderness of North America; birch bark canoes and unknown waterways and Indian captivity. The site of Minneapolis was one of the terminal points of this probing operation, but not much came of it at the time. No physical trace is left of this earliest phase. In some parts of the United States—particularly in the arid Southwest—the explorers and colonizers left monuments. They built missions and forts of stone and adobe brick that still stand as highwater marks of their advance. In timbered Minnesota, whatever log shelters may have existed are crumbled to mold in the intervening three centuries. Even later permanent monuments were deliberately destroyed: the stone watchtower at Fort Snelling was torn down a scant 60 years after it was erected.

Every school child knows that the Franciscan priest, Father Louis Hennepin, together with Michael Accault and Antoine Auguelle, was sent by the Sieur de la Salle to explore upstream of the newly-discovered Mississippi river. That was in late February, 1680. En route they were captured by a Sioux war-party and taken to the Indians' village on Lake Mille Lacs. It was not until July that Father Hennepin was permitted to explore further. He discovered the falls that he named St. Anthony. That was the future site of Minneapolis.

In his chronicles of the journey, Father Hennepin mentioned the falls almost casually. In 1695, Pierre Charles Le Sueur, a trader-explorer, revisited the falls and explored up the Minnesota river.

The first American to visit the locality was Captain Jonathon Carver of Connecticut who set out in 1766 to explore the territory ceded by France to Great Britain. He arrived at St. Anthony falls in November. He published a description calculated to warm the heart of any Chamber of Commerce:

"The country around the falls is extremely beautiful. It is not an uninterrupted plain where the eye finds no relief, but is composed of gentle ascents, which in summer are covered with the finest verdure and interspersed with little groves that give a pleasing variety to the prospect. On the whole, when the falls are included, which may be seen at a distance of four miles, a more pleasing and picturesque view cannot, I believe, be found throughout the universe."

Ensuing years saw little activity in the region save fur trading, but Minneapolis-to-be enjoyed some second-hand history with the American revolution which made everything east of the Mississippi a part of the United States. The western bank, which had been handed back and forth between France and Spain became American also with the Louisiana Purchase in 1803.

One can amuse oneself with the thought that things picked up after that—good old legendary American hustle.'

Lieutenant Zebulon M. Pike, in a less epic but companion expedition to that of Lewis and Clark, left St. Louis in 1805 to explore the headwaters of the Mississippi and other territories that the United States had just picked up at the bargain counter. In September, he arrived at the confluence of the Minnesota and Mississippi rivers, made a treaty with Sioux chiefs to purchase a tract nine miles square that included much of the present city of Minneapolis. Pike made the by-then-mandatory tourist trip to the falls. In fact, his party continued up the river to winter quarters in what is now Little Falls, Minnesota.

In 1817, Major Stephen H. Long arrived seeking a site for a military fortification that was to be Fort Snelling. He, of course, visited the falls. He had nothing but nice things to say: "The place were we encamped last night needs no embellishment to render it romantic in the highest degree . . . all contributed to render the scene the most interesting and magnificent of any I ever before witnessed."

It seems a pity that no forward-looking entrepreneur had established a soft-drink and postcard stand to handle all this starry-eyed trade.

Lieutenant Colonel Henry Leavenworth showed up in 1819 with a largish command to establish the fort. He was replaced the following spring by Colonel Josiah Snelling. The cornerstone of the first permanent building was laid on September 20, 1820. The post was called Fort St. Anthony until 1824, when the name was changed to Snelling.

It would be colorful to report that Fort Snelling contributed a glorious chapter to the history of American arms. Alas, however, such was not the case. It saw no battles or sieges. As it turned out, the fort's function was a peaceable one, but it served that function admirably.

Fort Snelling's job was not to do battle but to serve sentry duty. It was a kind of gate-warder to the wilderness extending north, south and west. The mere existence of the garrison established the white man's dominion over a vast unsettled area of forest and prairie. Merely by existing, Fort Snelling provided assurance and security and its existence encouraged prospective settlers, who arrived first in a trickle, then a freshet and finally in a flood.

The silent muskets and cannon at Fort Snelling thus only indirectly tamed the Minnesota territory. That was done by the settler's axe and plow—and to all practical purposes the domestication was accomplished in the space of barely 50 years.

It is interesting to note that almost immediately upon the establishment of Fort Snelling, two eminently unwarlike installations were constructed, both of them momentously symbolic of the future city.

In the autumn of 1820, a sawmill was built "a few rods" below St. Anthony falls to supply lumber for the military post. In 1823, a grist-mill was added to grind wheat that the soldiers had cultivated. This, of course, was the first use made of the falls' waterpower, subsequently to be exploited by a huge complex of sawmills and flour mills that were the principal factors in the physical and economic growth of Minneapolis.

Today's Betty Crocker would shudder at the reminiscences of Mrs. Ann Adams, who was 13 and living at the fort when the new mill went into operation:

"Colonel Snelling had sown some wheat that season and had it ground at a mill which the Government had built at the Falls; but the wheat had become moldy or sprouted and was dirty and it made wretched, black, bitter-tasting bread. This was issued to the troops, who got mad because they could not eat it and brought it to the parade ground and threw it down there. Colonel Snelling came out and remonstrated with them."

Strictly speaking, the first white civilian dwelling on the site of Minneapolis was that of Gideon and Samuel Pond, who in 1834 obtained permission from the military to establish an Indian mission on Fort Snelling land, officially closed to settlers. They built a log house atop a wooded knoll on the east side of Lake Calhoun, now Lakewood cemetery. Construction cost was one shilling, New York currency, for nails.

A year later, the Reverend J. D. Stevens arrived from New York to open a school for half-breed girls. The Ponds helped him build a house on the west shore of Lake Harriet.

A daughter was born to the Stevens that year—the first white child born outside the fort. And, in 1838, the first marriage on the site of Minneapolis was solemnized between Samuel Pond and Cordelia Eggleston, Mrs. Stevens' sister-in-law.

The question of settlement on the military reservation was a controversial one. In 1836, Major Joseph Plympton and two other garrison officers staked claims on the east side of the river—although it was not legal for officers on active duty to do so. Franklin Steele, a sutler on the post, knew this and in 1838 successfully "jumped" Plympton's claim, although he had no right to make a binding claim either since a treaty with the Chippewa Indians conveying the land to the United States had not yet been ratified. Nevertheless, he held out and eventually got the land.

Meanwhile, Plympton obtained war department authorization officially to set boundaries on the Fort Snelling reservation and evict all settlers within them. There were some 157 of these, all on the east side of the Mississippi river. Many left voluntarily and the rest were ordered driven out by bayonets in 1840, their cabins being burned by the soldiers.

The combination of delayed Indian treaties and restrictions on military land greatly delayed the founding of Minneapolis. Horace B. Hudson, in his 1908 history of the city observes that: ". . . Minneapolis, though standing on the most advantageous site for a city in the whole region, was retarded in development until practically the whole state of Minnesota had been opened to the immigrant."

With a touch of possibly partisan asperity, but with considerable logic, Hudson continued: ". . . had the upper part of the military reservation been opened for settlement in 1821, when Fort Snelling was founded, neither Mendota nor St. Paul would have been thought of. . . . And if a settlement had been made later at the site of St. Paul it would, in all probability, never have attained much importance."

Nevertheless, there continued a steady increase in inhabitants, informal claims and construction of shelters. There even was trade in the uncertain claims: Sergeant Nathaniel Carpenter, who had made an unofficial land claim to 320 acres adjoining Steele's, sold half interest to a Private Thomas Brown for $25 in 1838, whence it passed through other hands into those of Pierre Bottineau, a colorful character of French and Indian blood, in 1846.

Several squatters settled on the land and occupied it while resolutely awaiting government action that would legalize their holdings. Eli Pettijohn was one such who in 1842 claimed the site later occupied by the University of Minnesota.

In 1847 came the break-through—a United States land office was opened at St. Croix Falls to survey and distribute the land lying between the St. Croix and Mississippi rivers, then a part of the Wisconsin Territory. Immigration began in earnest.

This is not the place to detail the settlement of St. Anthony, as the community on the east bank of the river opposite the site of Minneapolis was named. But the names of some of the early settlers are familiar ones in the present city: Cummings, Dorr, Farnham, Godfrey, McDonald, Marshall, Russell, Tuttle, are a few that could be mentioned.

Ard Godfrey built the first civilian sawmill at the falls on Steele's land. It went into operation on September 1, 1848. That year, Roswell P. Russell built the first frame house in St. Anthony with lumber from the mill. He opened a store in the house, the first mercantile operation.

Mills and merchants. Already the stamp was upon the community, the size and prosperity of which has never ceased to grow in the 12 decades since.

Also in 1848, St. Anthony became official with completion of a government survey and plat. The population was then about 300. The town consisted of the lands of Steele, William A. Cheever and Bottineau, the latter of whom reportedly went to William R. Marshall, the platting surveyor, and said: "You jist take my land and fix him same lak M'sieu Steele land."

The fledgling town even got involved in an election that arose out of a strange set of circumstances. In that year, Wisconsin entered the Union as a state, but its boundary was fixed at the St. Croix river, not the Mississippi. Thus, St. Anthony, like the rest of the intervening region, found itself a no-mans-land.

It was felt that this left-over area was still the territory of Wisconsin, and so entitled to a delegate to Congress. A convention was called at Stillwater, where it was resolved to organize a new territory called Minnesota and meanwhile to elect a "Wisconsin" congressional delegate.

In the election, Henry H. Sibley defeated Henry M. Rice. It was a vigorous contest, to judge by a letter written by one William Dugas of St. Anthony: "Our election went of yesterday & considerable briefly we shold have don beter but they comence buying votes quite early in the Morning, this morning two young men was at my house and say that they was thretend to be kilt in the morning for saying hooraw for Sibley the other says they offerd him a dollar to vote for Rice but he answer that they were all his friends but that he shold vote for Sibley but he says now that before he voted he got verry

STATUE OF THOMAS LOWRY, HENNEPIN AND LYNDALE

MAIN STREET, UNDER THIRD AVENUE BRIDGE

Drunk and they changed his vote and consequently got a vot out of him for Rice when he entended to vote for Sibley. My Sellfe and all my friends around me have I believed save our money and not have offerd to any one pay for his vote."

Sibley's first act in Congress was to introduce a bill for the organization of the Minnesota Territory, which was passed and signed by President Polk on March 3, 1849. The stage was set for the genesis of Minneapolis proper —the occupation of those favored miles of gently rolling, wooded, lake-studded parkland stretching westward from the river that still is beautiful despite today's urban congestion, industrial districts or busy beetle-path streets. First, however, because of military and Indian treaty obstacles, a bit of gentle finagling was necessary.

As preface came the lease of the old government mill to Robert Smith in 1849. Smith never lived on the property, but the lease was a kind of bridgehead. That year there arrived at Fort Snelling a Vermonter named John H. Stevens who had been a captain in the Mexican war and who became chief clerk and confidant to Franklin Steele at the post. With Steele's encouragement and help, he set about securing a claim on the west bank, just above the mill. In what a 1923 historian, the Reverend Marion Daniel Shutter, called "a pleasing fiction," the Fort Snelling commandant and, through him, Secretary of War William Marcy were convinced that Stevens should be granted a claim on condition that he operate a ferry across the river—which could be forded (and dangerously) only at low water along a ledge near the falls at the foot of Nicollet island. The ferry would provide free crossing to all government troops, agents, wagons and the like traveling between Fort Snelling and Fort Gaines (later Fort Ripley).

Actually, Steele already had built a ferry from the upper end of Nicollet Island, but the new condition proved persuasive and Stevens was granted his request.

He began work on his house—the first residence of an actual settler in the city-to-be— in October, 1849, and he moved in with his bride from Illinois on August 6, 1850. It was a story-and-a-half frame farmhouse with a one-story kitchen wing. It stood on a shelf some 20 feet in elevation above the riverbank on the site of the present Great Northern Railroad depot at the foot of Hennepin Avenue. In 1855, Stevens received clear title to his claim.

It is not within the scope of this capsule account of the founding of Minneapolis to dwell minutely on the rapid surge across the river by subsequent settlers. Other military permits (not claims) were granted and, with the signing of the Treaty of Traverse des Sioux in 1851, several "sooners" staked claims in former Indian lands prior to the treaty's ratification and proclamation in early 1853.

In addition, there were numerous squatters who had moved onto the military and Indian lands with no pretense of permit or title. They were not typical of what the word "squatter" connotes, many being men of substance, education and prominence in the pioneer community.

Their action really attests to the unreality of the technical, even artificial, barriers so laggardly maintained between honest, industrious settlers and the pre-eminently desirable land otherwise lying fallow and unused. It is worthy of note that despite the influx of immigrants and consequent pressure for homestead sites, there is little evidence of land speculation or fortune-seeking among the earliest landholders.

In fact, the record is replete with cases of tracts given outright to new settlers or donated for public use in the growing community. Almost all the pioneer residents prospered, but this seems clearly to be the result of growing with the town they co-operatively

PLAQUE, FATHER HENNEPIN BLESSING WATERS OF ST. ANTHONY FALLS

worked to build, not merely of selfish greed or exploitation of newcomers.

Even an incomplete listing of some of these men of the 50's is interesting because their names are echoed today in Minneapolis street signs and parks and neighborhoods and institutions as well as being carried on by their descendants—among the city's leading families.

Ames, Ankeny, Atwater, Blaisdell, Folsom, Harmon, Hoag, Northrup, Basset, Case, Christmas, Fletcher, Franklin, Godfrey, Peters, Pratt, Stinson—even this brief, arbitrary roster tells the story.

At this point, the romantic portion of the chronicle nears its end. Minneapolis (still unnamed) was as yet a raw little settlement with no more than a dozen scattered houses, no government, no civic amenities, paveless streets and the most informal kind of commercial activity. Indian tepees still were pitched among the white man's buildings and the empty lands all about the settlement remained in their primordial state of nature.

ST. ANTHONY FALLS INDUSTRY, WASHINGTON AVENUE LOOKING SOUTH

Doctor Hezekiah Fletcher's claim—at what is now Portland Avenue and Fourteenth Street —was considered "away out in the country." But, even in the short-term view of the succeeding decade, the smallness of Minneapolis' beginnings are insignificant. It was no accident that the site was chosen and eagerly desired. Every factor argued that here should be a city.

It lay at the head of navigation of the Mississippi, that great communications vertebra of the continent. There was a seemingly limitless abundance of water power. It stood, literally, as the gateway to a vast, open empire of land that was quickly shown to be more fertile (because of its northerly latitude, not despite it) than many new regions opening up to the south.

The young nation was bursting out of its short pants. In 1820, about the time a few soldiers built the wilderness fort, the United States had a population of 9,500,000. By 1850, when Minneapolis still huddled in its mud, there were 23,000,000 Americans. In

SYTTENDE MAI CELEBRATION, LORING PARK

GODFREY HOUSE, UNIVERSITY AND THIRD AVENUE

SYTTENDE MAI

the next 10 years, the number had grown to 31,000,000, almost a one-third increase. It increased another third by 1870. And so on. Need and desire sent native Americans west. Events in troubled Europe of the mid-19th Century brought millions to our shores and large numbers of these headed west also, with no stopovers on the East Coast.

The process whereby Minneapolis and the new Minnesota territory filled with people was as simple and almost as commonplace as the filling of an empty basin when a water tap is turned on. There still were frontier adventures and hardships and bizarre events, but the growth would have occurred with or without melodrama.

The scene was crowded with remarkable individuals, with unusually gifted builders and organizers and leaders, but it also teemed with unnamed persons, who arrived seeking land and work, who found same and who did not thereafter lift their faces from their clerk's counters or sawhorses or trudging plows to be recognized. They pursued their simple lives and left their modest contributions as parts of the present, impressive whole.

The ensuing history of the city doubtless would have been written in similar characters regardless of the proportion between the vigorous developers and the steady toilers. Intuition suggests, however, that the city's peculiar modern character of energy, of open-mindedness, of congeniality towards intellectual, cultural and social advances is due to an unusually large percentage of able, intelligent and educated men among its pioneer population.

Perhaps it is not unique. After all, Minnesota and other frontier states of the time were not the Jamestown colony or any similar outpost on utterly alien soil. Its first settlers were primarily people from New England, Ohio, Illinois and other such stable, organized centers of population. They brought this stability with them and transplanted it in the form of pre-established institutions. Such people would not feel comfortable in any new community that did not have its library association or its Masonic lodge or all the trappings of county and city government or streets, sewers, fire departments and schools. They set about organizing these things as naturally as they laid foundation stones for their new homes.

Nonetheless, intuition still insists that certain special leavens were kneaded into the Minneapolis loaf. Perhaps it is pure economics that gave Minneapolis a livelier culture than, for example (and meaning no disparagement), Des Moines, Iowa, which is not as big nor as wealthy. Or maybe it was that Minneapolis started almost from scratch as a manufacturing town instead of being solely an agricultural marketplace, which might explain the premium set upon professional and technical training in addition to the businessman's shrewdness and the sturdy virtues of the farmer.

Minneapolis imported a tradition along with its brand-new citizens and since has embellished that tradition with local and self-generated ways of doing things. As a tradition, it may seem laughably short to European or even Eastern eyes, but it is not despicable.

One example of it is enough. In 1851, Calvin A. Tuttle moved across the river into Minneapolis; at the same time, he donated part of his east-bank claim as a site for a state university. In 1851, Minneapolis and St. Anthony together had less than 2,000 population. This handful of people, together with but a handful more scattered through an otherwise empty and echoing territory wanted a university. Before the year was out, they had one.

How is a city built? By building it. The chapter on venturesome explorer-priests and wilderness forts and lone cabins amid silent groves now is closed. The new chapter, although beginning more than a century ago, is wholly modern and more mundane.

One can entertain poetic thoughts about the ant-like toil that created the Pyramids or Inca temples atop Andean peaks, but there somehow is less flair in the work of building a modern city. Not even the most fanatic civic pride can be deeply moved to read that the first sewer in Minneapolis was commenced on June 15, 1871, yet sewers are needed and, like everything else that is needed in a growing city, they get built.

There are fat volumes of Minneapolis history that describe all these projects of civic necessity and improvement—no less important than the sewer, and many of them no more exciting. This section of our book is intended as no more than a glimpse of the city's origins and a hint of the natural advantages, grasped opportunities and citizen vigor that combined to spur the phenomenal growth of a backwoods village that got a very late start in life.

By 1900 (the year, incidentally, that John Stevens died), Minneapolis had become a modern, major city. In a scant 50 years, its population had increased tenfold to more than 200,000, doubling, tripling and quadrupling every decade; its assessed property valuation in 1922 had mounted to $266,-000,000—nearly ten times the price paid for the entire midcontinent in the Louisiana Purchase.

Neither its growth nor its history ended with 1900, of course, but these are mainly matters of living memory and some of them will be touched upon in other appropriate portions of this book. Let us close this account, then, with a brief chronology that might suggest the tempo of growth between 1850 and the close of the Nineteenth Century:

1849—First school in St. Anthony (Miss Electa Backus, teacher).

—First court convenes in St. Anthony (Judge Bradley B. Meeker).

1850—First steamboat, the Anthony Wayne,

FROM MILWAUKEE STATION

ascends river to Falls of St. Anthony.

—John H. Stevens occupies first permanent residence on west side of river.

1851—Territorial legislature establishes University of Minnesota. Preparatory school opens December 1.

—First newspaper, the St. Anthony Express, commences publication.

—First Odd Fellows lodge organized.

—Hennepin county established.

1852—First school on west side of river (Miss Mary E. Miller, teacher).

1854—First dray seen on city streets.

—First bank opens in St. Anthony (Richard Martin, president).

1855—Suspension bridge between St. Anthony and Minneapolis, first bridge to span the Mississippi, opened.

—St. Anthony incorporated as a city.

—Hennepin County Medical Society organized.

1856—Town of Minneapolis incorporated.

1857—First newspaper in Minneapolis, the Daily Falls Evening News, published.

1858—Minnesota admitted to the Union.

—The Nicollet House, first large hotel on west side of river, opens its doors.

1859—Minneapolis Athenaeum, forerunner to Public Library, is organized.

1865—First street grading in Minneapolis.

1866—Minneapolis YMCA organized.

1867—Minneapolis incorporated as a city.

—Police force organized.

—First city officers elected (Dorilus Morrison, mayor).

—Waterworks authorized.

1868—First fire companies in Minneapolis formed.

1870—Minneapolis Gas Light Company organized.

1871—First sewer (Huzzah!).

1872—St. Anthony and Minneapolis consolidated.

1878—Great explosion destroys seven large flour mills—and contributes to Minne-

apolis' decline as dominant milling city of the nation.

1881—Chamber of Commerce incorporated.

1882—Electric light introduced in Minneapolis—(N. B.: only thirty-two years after John Stevens built his house).

1886—Minneapolis School of Art founded.

1888—Minneapolis General Hospital authorized.

1889—City gets first electric streetcars.

1891—Cornerstone of present city hall and courthouse laid. (Completed 1905).

1892—Republican National Convention held in city.

1903—First concert of Minneapolis Symphony.

JOHN SARGENT PILLSBURY

BRONZE STATUE OF HIAWATHA AND MINNEHAHA, MINNEHAHA CREEK

CITY HALL

COUNCIL CHAMBERS

POLITICAL MEETING

REPUBLICAN HEADQUARTERS

ALDERMAN

FORMER CONGRESSMAN

STATE SENATOR

FORMER MAYOR

CAMPAIGN POSTERS

FATHER OF WATERS, CITY HALL

EVERY TOWN HAS A FACE. It is like an individual human face: partly inherited, partly the result of experience, partly the unconscious expression of character, partly the intentional visage offered to the world for approval.

The face of Minneapolis—or any town—is a complex of crowded and open places, architecture and streets and green patches and blight and beauty and odd, quirky, non-representative corners.

The basic Minneapolis face is an open one; it is nowhere a congested city. When its first few parcels of land were platted in the 1850s, the lines were drawn with the prairie-dweller's liberality with empty and plentiful land. This heritage gave us broad avenues and commodious side streets. Virtually all subsequent development held to this openness.

Even back in the Depression 30's, a WPA writers' project that did a guidebook on Minnesota (understandably tinged with the liberal social outlook of those days) points out that Minneapolis has no slums.

This is, in the largest sense, true. Minneapolis today has depressed areas of substandard housing, of inadequate or deleterious environment to be suffered by the adult residents and —worse—by the young people who necessarily study their place in the world upon the streets and sidewalks of their home territory. However, the worst Minneapolis neighborhood, whatever its privation of amenity, would seem resplendent to the warren-dwellers of eastern tenements or of bare-board, mud-street ghettoes of the south.

The most scabrous areas of the city, including the tumbledown Glenwood portions of Olson Highway, and the sad saloon-and-flophouse-and-pawnship reach of the Washington Avenue skidrow, have been leveled by urban redevelopment. Public housing in the Glenwood area replaced rotting wood with cinderblock and brick. No one could trumpet any triumph of graciousness, but even the barracks-like units and the flatfaced high-rises are distributed widely among green lawns and playgrounds.

The Lower Loop area, ex-Skidrow, existed for several years as a razer's wasteland of parking lots and flattened rubble, but now is being steadily peopled with new business buildings.

There still are depressing areas. East of the downtown section in the 'teen avenues from Washington to Franklin Avenues are unkempt dwellings and rooming houses (primarily Negro and Indian) that bespeak the shame of high rent and low upkeep.

Across the river are long stretches of southeast and northeast Minneapolis streets lined with houses that are sound and safe and sanitary but dreary with that awful, square, peaked-roof, uniform dreariness that was the 1920s' ill-advised contribution to the American architectural scene.

Eastern Franklin Avenue and a six-block portion of upper Nicollet Avenue inherited at least part of the former skidrow's dubious function, confirming the predictions of expert witnesses during Lower Loop redevelopment hearings who pointed out that any major city will have its share of transients, casual laborers, family-less pensioners and socially dispossessed persons who require (and who is to say do not deserve?) cheap food, cheap beds and cheap amusements, including liquor. These are the blemishes on the face of Minneapolis and should be acknowledged. The face-in-whole, however, is fair. It may not be as fair as those of us who like it would contend, but the most impartial observer would agree that it is fair enough.

It is not best judged by the immediate aspect of the downtown area. The broadness of the streets works always in the city's favor, but

RIVER INDUSTRIAL AREA, NORTH WASHINGTON

even they have a seasonal drawback when scouring winter wind and snow make one wish perhaps for something a bit more constricted, angular and cozy. Charming quaintness we ain't got.

Downtown architecture defies classification —except perhaps as Midwest Motley. The bulk of buildings are of the vintages from the 1880s through the 1920s and, if they were not so staid, might be said stylistically to run riot. It is all there: sandstone Victorian, marble Greek Revival, bland, brick Babbitt Baroque. There even is a former bank building modeled after an Egyptian temple with deep-carved hieroglyphics about its doorway. These are no better and no worse than other cities have to offer. Change is taking place— and it is in all likelihood no better and no worse, either.

Within the past ten years, there has been something between a five and fifteen per cent replacement of public and commercial buildings in Minneapolis proper, plus extensive refurbishing of older structures.

The renewal has eliminated many architectural infirmities and several downright outrages, but also cost the city one of the unique buildings in the nation—the old Metropolitan Life building, built in the mid-1880s. It was the first skyscraper west of the Mississippi. To modern tastes, it was a self-conscious atrocity on the outside, but a dramatic fairyland inside with its vast twelve-story central well, ringed by a tracery of brass-railed, glass-floored interior balconies.

The new buildings range from the now-standard glass-and-aluminum glossiness of the towering First National Bank building and the more modest Lutheran Brotherhood to the squinty-windowed cubes of the brand-new Northern States Power and IBM buildings in the Lower Loop restoration.

For myself, at any rate, the glowing jewel of them all is the just-finished Northwestern National Life building by Minoru Yamasaki, a structure of delicious drama and gracefulness that seems to float amid its park-like setting on airy, slender arches and yet is substantial and solid with its flat roof line and deep-pillared portico.

Just as every family has a disreputable relative somewhere, every city has its prominent architectural oddity. Minneapolis' is the Foshay Tower, the dreamchild of one Wilbur Foshay who erected an investment and utilities empire in the post-World War I era. The empire proved so shaky that Foshay went to prison, but the building he dedicated in 1929 (of all years!) as a monument to himself and George Washington still is with us. It is a great ungainly pylon that somehow is both too squat and too skinny and is perforated with an improbable number of windows. The esthetic judgment of the structure is best expressed in the joke: "Why is it worth fifty cents to go to the top of the Foshay Tower?" "Because that is the only place in town where you can't see the Foshay Tower." To stroll downtown Minneapolis is to encounter few especial delights or surprises to the eye, although most of the store and building fronts at street level are handsomely enough turned out or, at the very least, inoffensive.

Nevertheless, there are numerous cheerful innovations being made. Sunken terraces provide the approaches to the Sheraton-Ritz Hotel and the Northern States building. Graceful, enclosed second-story walkways span Marquette Avenue and Seventh Street to connect the new Northstar Center with the Northwestern National Bank and Roanoke buildings (the Northstar owners still hope for approval of a plan to suspend a restaurant above the entire intersection of those thoroughfares). And, of course, planning has been approved for the Nicollet Mall, a landscaped, traffic-free pedestrian way that will extend some eight blocks through that avenue's principal shopping section.

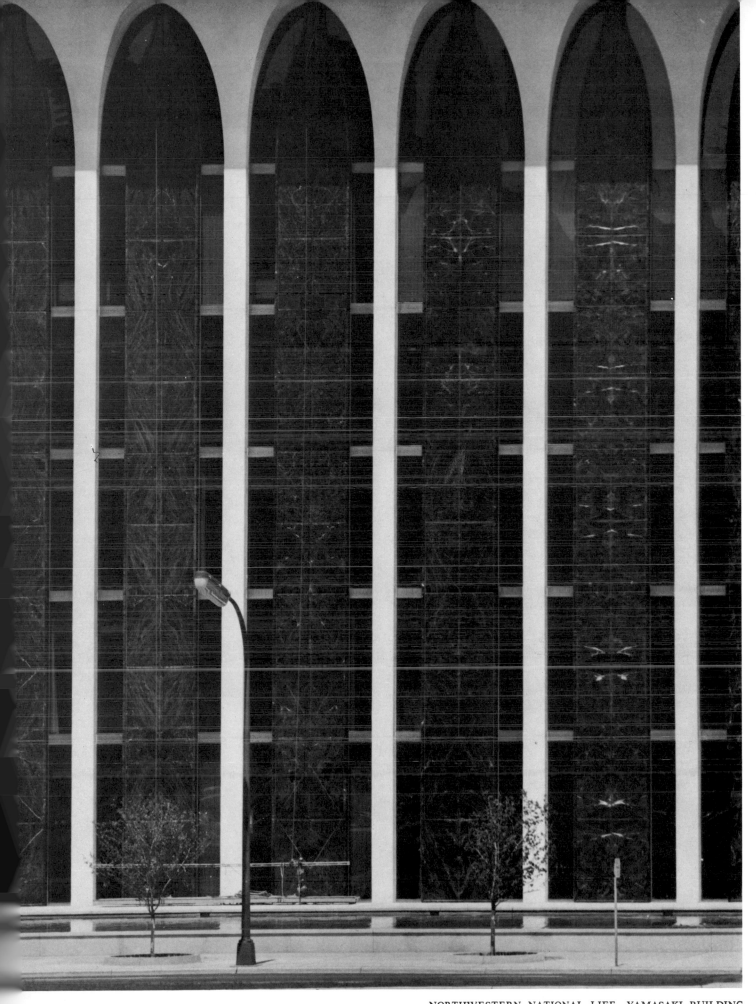

NORTHWESTERN NATIONAL LIFE, YAMASAKI BUILDING

Topography does not permit Minneapolis any such drama as San Francisco's hills and harbor, but our city has worked consciously to exploit its own impressive potential for beauty. The Lower Loop development, the Nicollet Mall and hopes for salvaging the neglected river front are signs that similar beauties may be achieved for the busy, workaday downtown district.

The residential areas are the city's glory and have a special interest in that they do not, as elsewhere, offer isolated clusters of handsome homes and streets, but rather flow in long, looping bands through the length and breadth of the town. A Sunday driver can start downtown and circle the entire city along parkways and lake drives and river roads lined with felicitious homes of every vintage—and of every size from magnificent to snugly modest. Between these well-favored homesites, to be sure, are flat, grid-like streets of unimaginative, utilitarian domestic architecture common to every city. Nonetheless, the relative proportions of pretty to plain is in Minneapolis advantageously high on the side of pretty.

Save for the mentioned depressed areas (a small fraction of the whole) the level of tidy upkeep in any Minneapolis neighborhood is impressive. It is indeed a residential city and its worst sins are patches of real estate that seem dull in contrast to abundant beauties on either side. With rare exception, neglect and decay are not the ruling process.

A good example of this is the Kenwood district, which lies on the southwestern verge of the downtown area and which at the turn of the century was a chosen neighborhood of the upper middle class. Accidents of geography and traffic patterns preserved Kenwood from the encroachment of commercial interests, but with passing generations many of its big old homes were reduced to rooming houses. Since World War II, however, growing younger families started moving back into

SHERATON RITZ HOTEL

FOSHAY TOWER

the area in search of the inexpensive spaciousness of these houses.

The result is that Kenwood has almost completely been restored—its quiet, tree-lined streets teeming with young children, its houses refurbished and made charming again with loving care. Few cities can boast so interesting an exhibit of domestic architecture — not fossilized, but still serving the original purposes for which the homes were built.

The fun of walking or driving through an area like Kenwood is the profusion and variety of styles. There are homes of classic beauty, there are grotesque abortions that would make Charles Addams laugh, there are quaint, quirky scrimshawed homes that some proud 1890 banker or merchant put up like a banner announcing his success. But, in present-day Kenwood, all of these houses are loved for themselves like an eccentric great uncle, and residents may take special pride in the fact that his house is nuttier than any other on the block.

Owners devotedly restore the old wood paneling and carving in big, high-ceilinged rooms. They delight in stained-glass windows and the extravagance of odd-shaped alcoves and music rooms and pantries. Antiquated pipes and wiring and furnaces must be replaced with new, but the graciousness of the whole is studiedly retained. This isn't wise-apple Camp; this is a pleasant way to live.

In some areas of Minneapolis, past glories are irredeemably lost. Park Avenue, for example, once was the Midwest equivalent of its New York namesake — a street of castled wealth — but the city's commercial expansion blindly engulfed it. Now, most of its mansions, whether tastefully grand Georgian townhouses or ghastly, furbelowed replicas of Rhine castles, have been taken over by insurance offices, charitable and church organizations and the like.

Around each of the baker's dozen of larger

WINTER

SUBURB

FROM OLD MANSION, PARK AVENUE

THETA DELTA CHI, UNIVERSITY OF MINNESOTA

lakes in the city proper and the scores that dot the western suburbs are homes and neighborhoods appropriate to their setting. These are not the exclusive preserve of the economically privileged, but of every class: there is enough natural beauty in Minneapolis for all.

The main thrust of Minneapolis' growth was due south from the falls of St. Anthony, where the city was born. This movement was parallel to the Mississippi's course and extended past the slightly rolling land to Minnehaha creek and onto the flat plateau that now comprises the suburban cities of Richfield and Bloomington. This area was particularly well-suited to mass-produced housing after the war and inevitably it suffers somewhat from the uniformity of huge tract developments.

Growth north and west was slower historically, but, since the metropolitan area reached its natural boundary at the Minnesota river, expansion turned in these directions. Sparse rural townships to the north with scattered farms and crossroad general stores (such as Crystal or Brooklyn Center or Plymouth), have grown to large population centers within a bare two decades. To the west, the attractively rolling, wooded terrain of Golden Valley, St. Louis Park, Hopkins, western Edina and, latterly, exurban Eden Prairie have filled in at some places to near-urban density. Lake Minnetonka, whose huge expanse of water, of countless bays and inlets and miles of shoreline formerly made it the city's summer resort, now is settled in solidly with people who do not consider themselves commuters despite the 15 or 20 miles they must drive one way to get to their jobs in Minneapolis.

In postwar England, urban planning received urgent attention. The rebuilding of blitzed cities suggested the possibility of doing something about the congestion and clutter that had accumulated over the centuries. One solution was the building of "New Towns" that would radiate concentrically from the central city and communicate with it, but which would each be separated by a "green belt" of open land and breathing space.

Minneapolis is fortunate in that the natural features of its site and the conditions of its growth produced something very like the above ideal. With an assist from the merciful foresight of earlier park board officials, the phenomenally rapid growth of the city somehow did not strangle itself or destroy its natural advantages. Rivers, lakes, creeks, parkways, extended stretches of broken or low-lying ground not immediately practicable for building almost automatically created a series of green belts. Also, the openness of the country surrounding the new city led to a naturally radial plan, whereby suburbs could grow up all around the compass of Minneapolis (and, of course, St. Paul) and all be roughly equidistant from the cities' centers.

Now, with some one-and-a-half million population in the Twin Cities area, the traumas common to metropolitan life in most other centers are mild where they are not non-existent. Minneapolitans complain of rush-hour traffic, but relative to other metropolises, it hardly deserves the name. Suburban populations are uniformly distributed around Minneapolis, not assymetrically concentrated in a few quarters.

Only in the most recent years has the need been felt to build freeway arteries to handle traffic and even now (if a former commuter can express a personal opinion) they are more of a luxury than a necessity: they will shave five to fifteen minutes off travel time for the average suburbanite. But he was getting to work with comparative convenience before the freeway program started.

Minneapolis, hemmed within fixed boundaries, remains stable (in fact, its population declined by about four thousand from 1960 to 1965), but its satellite suburbs and those of St. Paul are booming at an increasing pace: up by an estimated 211,000 persons in the same five-year period. That is more than 13 per cent.

There is ample room for it. Without crowding. Without losing the metropolis' characteristic color of green. Within the foreseeable future, at least, Minneapolis will keep its open face.

LAKE CALHOUN

INTERIOR, TURN OF CENTURY HOME

FIRST NATIONAL BANK

METROPOLITAN BUILDING BEING DEMOLISHED

NO SINGLE FACE can be called typical of any American city—not after a century of change and interchange.

The popular imagination, however, is not entirely wide of the mark when it visualizes certain archetypical figures at the mention of place names. Say "Milwaukee" and a portly, beer-drinking German burgher springs to mind. "New York" conjures up a sharp-eyed, sharp-tongued cabdriver. "Dallas" is a tall, Stetsoned cowpoke who happens to be prospering as a businessman.

These types are more noticeable than others who may be the actual statistical representatives of their city's populace. But, as symbols they are not wholly inappropriate — if only because they often are that city's own image of itself.

Say "Minneapolis" and the outsider might automatically think "Swede." Whatever affront this reflex might offer Norwegians, it is not hopelessly false. Don't blame me. Go ask the United States Bureau of Census.

The 1960 census defines "foreign stock" as being the foreign-born population combined with native-born of foreign parentage on either side. This includes all first and second-generation Americans.

Taking Hennepin county, which closely approximates the greater Minneapolis metropolitan area and excludes that of St. Paul, the last census showed a total population of 842,000 (rounding off the figures) of which 620,000 were of native parentage and 222,-000, or 25 per cent, were foreign stock.

But, it should be borne in mind that third and subsequent generations are considered native stock regardless of family origins and that, back in 1880, the census reported 71 per cent of all Minnesotans as being Europeans of the first and second generations. Hence, figures for the present day can be considered to reflect also the heritage represented by third and fourth generations.

In Hennepin county now, nearly 52,000 of

the foreign stock is Swedish. That is more than 23 per cent.

In addition, 16.5 per cent is Norwegian. This brings us to the perilous brink of the keen distinctions Swedes and Norwegians (and Danes) quite properly make about their national ancestry. From this, the prudent non-Scandinavian quickly recoils—although many persons elsewhere do not trouble with the vital differences. Even a few of us locals who should know better sometimes step on proud Scandinavian toes.

At present, the total Scandinavian contribution to the Minneapolis area's foreign stock comprises about 42.5 per cent. When you consider that in the 1880s, no less than 50 per cent of the state's foreign-born population was Scandinavian, it becomes plain a huge number of their descendants are listed now as native-born.

Small wonder that the rest of the country thinks of Minneapolis as peopled by blue-eyed blonds.

Yet Minneapolis is no Stockholm or Olso. More than any other national groups, according to students of the great 50-year wave of immigration that fleshed out and filled the Minnesota wilderness, the Scandinavians were the quickest to assimilate themselves into the ways and traditions of their new home.

Also, 50 per cent is only half the story. The first tide of settlers were native Yankees from New England, New York, Pennsylvania and the already developed Midwestern states. French and British drifted down from Canada in great numbers. As the territory's boundless opportunities opened up, there was great need for lumbering, railroad, farm and construction labor. Intense salesmanship efforts were launched in northern Europe to recruit immigrants. The state, as well as industrial developers and even individual towns and counties, papered the Old World with pamphlets, posters and newspaper articles extolling the wonders of the new territory.

PICNIC, MINNEHAHA PARK

DAYTON'S WINDOW, CHRISTMAS

WALKER ART CENTER, CHILDREN'S EXHIBIT

MOTHER AND CHILD, NICOLLET ISLAND

Political, social and religious unrest were particularly strong in mid-19th Century Sweden and Germany and it is not surprising that these nations produced the greatest immigrant response. Up until 1900, Germany led in the export, then Sweden pulled ahead. This was fortunate for the new state, since the peoples of these countries, even those of humble station, were exceptionally literate, socially stable and diligent. They also were particularly grateful for the unrigidified personal freedom they found.

The rapid expansion of the state's economy, as well as the continued flow of newcomers quickly elevated earlier arrivals into the middle class and shortened the process whereby a European peasant might be forced by conditions in crowded Eastern cities to remain a European peasant—despite his ocean crossing.

The Irish arrived in great numbers through the peak influx of 1890, following which there was a wave of "new immigration" by Finns and Slavs, most of whom were brought over to work the developing iron mines of the north. By 1900, the meat packing industry in the southern parts of the state was recruiting Balkan, Polish and Lithuanian labor. These latter groups tended to remain regionally concentrated, but, of course, Minneapolis received some proportional increment of each.

It is cliche to speak of the American melting pot. Nevertheless, historical factors make the phrase peculiarly valid in Minnesota and in its largest city. The relatively brief period during which the state was settled, the wide-open economy and social mobility that prevailed here vastly speeded the work of assimilation. Not even in formerly homogenous settlements like New Ulm, New Prague or Vasa, Minnesota, do you now hear the German or Swedish that once was the common tongue. Even less so have ethnic groups in Minneapolis clung to their old ways.

This is not to say that all heritages of the European past have been abandoned. On the contrary, it is fair to surmise that this city's peculiar richness of cultural life is directly due to the variety of traditions that have endured beneath so recently acquired an American overlay. But, the good thing is that these traditions have been to a great extent intermingled and shared, not confined within isolated ethnic clusters.

Minneapolitans of every national origin flock to the fabulous annual feast served by the Greek Orthodox church on Lake Calhoun. Irish and Scandinavians alike enjoy the sumptuous, authentic Sunday smorgasbord at the Sons of Norway lodge headquarters. La Casa Coronado Restaurant, which used to be located amid St. Paul's small Mexican community, recently and most successfully moved to Minneapolis—which has less than half as many Mexican residents.

National holidays, such as the Swedish Svenskarnas Dag or the Norwegian Syttende Mai, are items of city-wide interest, whether other national groups participate or not.

There is danger here of painting too rosy a picture of loving brotherhood down through the decades. Minneapolis was not immune to prejudice and injustice toward minorities. Not only did the Europeans bring their national animosities with them, but were themselves greeted by native American intolerance of aliens.

Many of the worst effects of this were ameliorated, however, by the fact that the immigrants were needed and wanted in the days when there was much work to do and too few hands to do it. Barring times of cyclic depression, the native Minnesotan felt relatively little economic threat from foreign labor.

Nonetheless, there are shameful chapters. In the 20's and 30's, Minneapolis had the unsavory reputation as a center of anti-Semitic feeling. There was social and economic ostracism. Jews for the most part lived in their

RABBI AND CONGREGATION

YOUNG BOY

own neighborhoods—on the North Side and in the Seven Corners area to the east.

Remnants of anti-Semitism still are to be encountered (as elsewhere) among the unthinking, but (as elsewhere) there has been a general abatement of such ugly prejudice. Jews now figure prominently among the civic, cultural, philanthropic, intellectual and professional leadership of Minneapolis. The present mayor is of Jewish descent.

The Negro minority in Minneapolis is a changing one. Until recent years, the city and state numbered few Negro residents. In 1850, there were but 39; in 1950, there were 14,022. The 1960 census reports 22,263 Negroes out of a total state population of 3,413,864, more than a 50 per cent increase.

Of these, about 11,700 live in the greater Minneapolis area—roughly 1.4 per cent of the total 842,000 Hennepin county population. Minneapolis Negroes encounter no formal segregation in education, housing or employment—in fact there are official commissions and legislation against discrimination. Visible and tacit inequalities do exist, but apparently to a less severe degree than prevails in other Northern cities with larger Negro communities.

The only figures available are for the combined Minneapolis-St. Paul area, but they show residents of foreign stock from more than a hundred nations around the globe, including Albania (8), Argentina (90), The Azores (11), Australia (339) and South Africa (77).

What is the object in dwelling thus on ethnic distribution, which doubtless differ from other cities only by a few decimal points shifted slightly to right or left? The point has been made that this area had a consistently higher rate of foreign immigration than any other frontier region. But, the point also has been made that assimilation was uniquely successful.

Minneapolitans today are basically no different in their pleasures, problems and pursuits than the people of other American cities. And yet, all communities have their own distinctive personalities. That of Minneapolis surely proceeds as much from the rapidity and intensity with which broadly diverse races, nationalities and cultures came together as it does from purely local economic or geographic or climatic factors.

Personality is too intangible a thing to attempt to define in words—the pictures in this book of the people of Minneapolis and the ways they live can give a much better hint of that elusive essence.

But, who is the average Minneapolitan—that sturdy statistical fiction that can be chopped up into tenths and still survive?

He or she has a median age of 29.2. He or she has grown young by 2.7 years since 1950, which is nice for her. They also have acquired 24 per cent more fellow statistics in the greater Minneapolis area during the past decade.

Of 209,448 families, 4,286 have incomes under $1,000 a year; an almost equal number, 4,228 have incomes over $25,000. The family median income is $6,954.

Occupationally, there are more white collars than blue or any other shade. There are 340,196 persons of both sexes reported employed by the 1960 census. The occupational breakdown is of interest:

In the general category of professional, technical, engineering, medical, health, teaching and kindred vocations, are recorded 48,654 persons—that is, about 14 per cent.

Of managers, officials and proprietors (excluding the small farm group of 1,423), there are 31,962—a bit over 9 per cent.

Clerical, sales and kindred occupations account for 90,076 (26 percent). Service jobs number 31,204 (9 per cent). These vocational groups come roughly to 58 per cent of the work force.

Craftsmen, foremen and kindred manufacturing and construction jobs total 43,007 (12 per cent). So-called operatives (semiskilled and other machine workers), plus drivers and the like, number 47,123 (14 per cent) and laborers, totaling 11,843, are a bare 3 per cent. Assorted other jobs make up the balance.

Skilled, prosperous, well-educated, stable (Minneapolis ranks among the top cities of the nation in home-ownership, savings, credit and "staying put") these are the people who make up a city. No two are alike, perhaps, but it seems that what they like they have found here.

FOLK CELEBRATION, LORING PARK

BOY AND GIRL

HIAWATHA AND MINNEHAHA

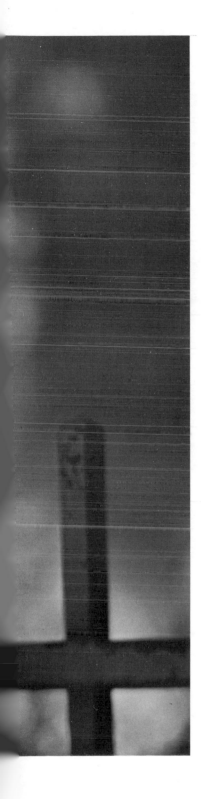

IN THE RHYTHM OF THE SEASONS, summer in Minneapolis is the andante movement. With feeling.

Commerce and industry still rear their ugly visages and we all must trudge off to the office or shop to earn a living, but our strongest impulse is to bask lizard-like in the sun. We do so at every opportunity and on the slightest pretext. Ours is not the heat-sodden lethargy of a southern summer. It is more a time of langorous self-congratulation, of shamelessly indulgent well-being.

Barring one, or at the most two, week's worth of swelter when hot and humid Great Plains air settles over the city, Minneapolis summers are delightfully congenial visitors that never outstay their welcome. Average monthly temperatures are: June, 68; July, 73; August, 71, and September, 62. But, even at 90 and above, it would take a chronic malcontent to complain of the heat—the lack of which he complained of during the winter.

Summer is a time of near-frenzy for golfers—of whom the city seems provided in almost indecent numbers (there are 30 golf courses in the metropolitan area). As a non-golfer, I must confess, I undergo certain conversational trials since most of my friends and associates will talk of little else from May through September. Oh well, it is not much worse than the baseball season: as a non-fan, my dialogue is equally limited.

Or, the fishing season. Next to golf, I would guess, fishing incites more fanaticism than any other summer activity. The anglers descend in veritable battalions upon every lake in or near the city every week-end—or travel further afield to northern Minnesota waters. I don't fish and so am denied the opportunity to join in the superabundant mendacity that passes for discourse among those who do.

PAN FISH

ELOISE BUTLER WILD FLOWER GARDEN

GREAT NORTHERN DEPOT

AQUATENNIAL QUEEN

MINNEHAHA CREEK

BEACH IN SUMMER

PICNIC

MINNESOTA TWINS

Or the boaters. Increasingly, Minneapolitans are expending their leisure and affluence on power craft, armadas of which ply the adjacent lakes and rivers every summer. Water-skiing, marine hot-rodding or lazy cruising dominate the life of thousands. I don't happen to fancy motor boats, which debars me from another topic of conversation. Fortunately, I used to sail in my youth and there is a large contingent with whom I can exchange gossip about halyards and spinnakers and such like matters.

The stranger might well ask what good is summer to me, an indolent slob who partakes of none of these wholesome activities. They miss the point.

Summer is the most glorious time of the year in which to do nothing at all. My deepest urge is simply to roll on my back under the luxuriant warmth of the sun like a kitten on a hearth. This being unseemly conduct for a middle-aged man, I have found other outlets for my do-nothingism.

I might, for example, sit in the sun on an upstairs back porch, reading a book and sipping gin and tonic. Or, I may sit in the gentle breezes on a shaded front porch and sip gin and tonic while reading a book. Or I may sit in the yard with a book and a glass. At times, I find it agreeable to hunt up a neighbor who is sitting on his outdoor terrace and join him in a gin and tonic. In short, the possibilities for summer enjoyment are almost limitless.

Should I experience an upsurge of energy, a leisurely stroll of about five blocks takes me to one of the beautiful lakes that lie in the heart of the city. If the hike proves exhausting, I can sit on the shore and meditate upon such topics as the futility of human exertion. Or, if my vital juices are still aflow, a walk around the lake more than repays the effort.

The northern latitude of Minneapolis exacts its toll in winter, but repays any outrage by the increased length of lovely summer days. With daylight saving, sunset is not until nine p.m. for much of the summer. Whatever harrassments have plagued your work day, you can come home in the comforting knowledge that there still are hours ahead in which you may relax in outdoor sunlight — and linger long after supper to enjoy the soft, gently-fading twilight.

After business hours on a work day, the city's 15 bathing beaches are crowded with individuals, couples and families having a swim or a loll in the sun. On week-ends, the natatorial activity is even heavier and remains so daylong. Owing to the many lakes and beaches that are available, however, you seldom encounter the jam-packed density of swimmers that make similar beaches in other big cities resemble a seal rookery.

When one rhapsodizes summer pleasures in Minneapolis, it should be done in grateful memory of those visionaries more than eighty years ago who foresaw a future need and provided for it. They and the citizens since who preserved and enlarged their vision assured for Minneapolis the remarkable number and size of public parks and lakes that enable us to enjoy our precious days of sun and warmth in uncongested comfort.

The first park in the city was donated in 1857 by Edward Murphy, a pioneer developer. The two blocks between Twenty-Second and Twenty-Third Avenues South, near Franklin Avenue, still is called Murphy Square. For years, it was used as a cow pasture, but in 1873, Murphy got city council approval of a five hundred dollar appropriation to fence and landscape the park. The mayor, however, refused to repay Murphy.

Such niggardliness was typical of the city government at the time. Early plans to obtain land for city parks on Nicollet Island (37 acres), near Grant Street (20 acres), on Nicollet Avenue between Franklin and Twenty-Fourth Street (40 acres) and an extensive part of

Lake Harriet shore (250 acres) all were stifled by city hall politics and pinch-purse protesters —one of whom argued that there would never be any houses south of Tenth Street, so why bother with parks?

But, there were other voices. In 1880, the Minneapolis Tribune declared in an editorial: "We regret that Minneapolis is more in need of a park than ever, now that it has a band to discourse agreeable music on fine summer evenings. The appropriation for a pleasure ground of a suitable area of land as near the heart of town as possible should not be put off another day. The longer the matter is delayed, the more difficult and expensive it becomes. . . . If we had but a few acres where our citizens could congregate on festal occasions for open air assemblies, it would be an invaluable possession. . . . We suggest that Minneapolitans make a vow never to fire off another rocket nor gratify themselves with the sound of orchestral music or indulge in any sort of civic merry-making until the municipality has furnished a fitting spot, with green turf under foot, with arching boughs overhead and Heaven's big dome above in which there will be room for all to come together in a free communion of cheeriness and gay humor."

Such agitation led the privately-organized Board of Trade to initiate enabling legislation for a Minneapolis Park Board with taxing powers. Predictably, the city council opposed the measure and the Knights of Labor protested that by this "iniquitous measure" the "door is left open to rob the working classes of their homes and make driveways for the rich at the expense of the poor." Nonetheless the park act was ratified in a city-wide vote, 5,327 to 3,992, and the first Minneapolis Park Board convened in March of 1883, with Charles M. Loring as president—commencing a term of service that earned him the honorific of "father of the park system."

Almost immediately, a far-seeing plan for an ambitious park system was approved, based upon suggestions by H. W. S. Cleveland, a landscape gardener who urged broad, tree-lined avenues (handy as firebreaks, also, he pointed out), acquisition and development for public enjoyment of all lake and river shores within the city, and timely measures to secure open land for parks in anticipation of population growth.

It is impossible to recount all subsequent details, but it is significant that negotiations to acquire Lake Harriet and a public right of way around it were opened the same year the Park Board came into existence. During that first year, in fact, 20 acres of Riverside Park along the Mississippi, plus the tracts that now are called Loring, Logan and Fairview parks, were purchased.

Thenceforward, until the present size and range of the park system had been achieved, hardly a year went by without additional purchases and donations of land to expand existing properties or to create new parksites throughout the city. At present, Minneapolis has 153 parks totaling almost six thousand acres—an area equal in size to the entire city of Bemidji, Minnesota. There is one acre of park for every 80 inhabitants of Minneapolis. There also is a playground for every square mile of residential area.

One of the most imaginative concepts of the nineteenth century park planners was a "Grand Round" of scenic parkways encircling the city. In the days of carriages, these might have been construed as "driveways for the rich at the expense of the poor," but the Knights of Labor protest could not survive the quickly apparent fact that these parkways were for the pleasure of all. Succeeding Park Boards painstakingly strung together parcels of land, surfaced roadways and broad, landscaped belts until the circle was completed. Subsequent developments of heavy auto traffic patterns and the changed character of neighborhoods has opened up about a three-mile gap in the ring in northeast Minneapolis, but today's motorist can start on St. Anthony Boulevard, thence along Victory Memorial Drive and Glenwood Parkway to make a circuit of the lake district—Cedar, Lake of the Isles, Calhoun and Harriet, follow beautiful Minnehaha Parkway to Minnehaha Falls and the river and then up the River Road to the University. This continuous circuit of more than thirty-five miles is a charming drive through uniformly handsome surroundings. There is no equivalent system in any other American city.

The 22 lakes within the city limits, for which Minneapolis is famous, did not happen by accident. Although they existed naturally (as geological remnants of the pre-glacial course of the Mississippi river) their present beauty and utility is the result of the Park Board's desire to have them so.

Until improved, they were unkempt bodies of water mostly surrounded by barriers of swamp. For example, between 1911 and 1925, more than a quarter-million dollars was spent dredging 1.3 million cubic yards of

LAKE HARRIET BEACH

swamp mud to fill in marshy areas and create the present shoreline of Lake Calhoun. Early photographs of Lake of the Isles, now one of the city's most beautiful ornaments, show it surrounded by cattail bogs more suitable for duck-hunters than the strollers and picnickers who enjoy its dreaming lawns, shade trees and footpaths today.

It might have startled the economy-minded park opponents of 1883 to know that all of these improvements have more than paid for themselves: $300,000 was spent to beautify Lake of the Isles, for instance, but almost immediately the value of adjoining real estate increased 100 to 500 per cent. The same has been true everywhere in the city. Esthetic and recreational values create dollars-and-cents values—and the city as a whole has benefitted economically from its planned program of self-beautification.

Summer is a time dear to youth—and grown-ups can think back to their own childhood days of sunny freedom and fun. There is a charming account of a civic celebration in

1911 to be found in a history of the Minneapolis park system by Theodore Wirth—the park superintendent who from 1906 to 1935 was the real artist who brought the vision to pass. There is a touching innocence and youthful enthusiasm about the event that would be inconceivable today.

The occasion was the opening of a channel connecting Lake of the Isles with Lake Calhoun. This was considered important enough for a weeklong festival. Downtown, there were hanging gardens and arches. The state militia paraded and played concerts. Up to 150,000 people watched a "Water Parade" by the Lake Harriet Canoe Club. On the big day, the waters of the joined lakes were mingled symbolically in a gold loving cup. A steam launch carrying officials made the first passage between the lakes, followed by a fleet of decorated craft. My favorite portion of the festival is this—to quote Mr. Wirth:

"That evening, Lake of the Isles was the scene of a brilliant parade of illuminated Ships of All Ages, a very beautiful spectacle

LAKE HARRIET

— novel and educational — in which 170 canoes participated, together with the Women's Rowing Club with a chain of 30 rowboats. A throne had been erected on a platform on the larger of the two islands of the lake, and here five young women in appropriate costumes, impersonating the spirits of Minneapolis, Lake Harriet, Lake of the Isles, Cedar Lake and Lake Calhoun, reviewed the parade of ships — replicas of ancient water craft illuminated and manned by crews in picturesque historical costumes. The island was also attractively illuminated and after the parade, a brilliant display of fireworks climaxed the eventful day."

In our sophistication, we chuckle at such simple edification—but in 1911 it obviously was real and satisfying to the citizenry. We may reflect, without false nostalgia, that possibly we moderns have lost something rather nice. Whatever the case, it was this kind of enthusiasm that created our parks — where summer in Minneapolis is seen at its radiant best.

LAKE OF THE ISLES

*U*NTIL I MOVED TO MINNEAPOLIS, I had never heard of a storm window. For all I knew, it was something like the eye of a hurricane.

I soon discovered what a storm window is. A storm window is a device invented by wives to assure that no husband shall enjoy autumn. Leaving it to the abnormal psychologists to explain why wives cannot tolerate husbandly pleasure, let me explain storm windows for the benefit of anyone who may not know (a Tennessee Williams character, perhaps) and into whose hands this book might fall.

A storm window is a secondary or ancillary glazed sash affixed, appended or otherwise superimposed upon the permanent window of a dwelling. Its purpose is to provide additional protection against wintry cold, decrease heat loss and increase the divorce rate.

As the ancients must have walked in superstitious dread of recurring plague or the septennial swarming of locusts, so do Minnesota husbands feel their mouths go dry and their stomach muscles tighten every autumn at the looming prospect of putting up the storm windows.

The uninitiated might well be perplexed. What, I can hear the uninitiated ask, is so bad about putting up storm windows? It is stupid questions like that which keep these people uninitiated.

They fail to perceive that before one can put up storm windows, one must first remove the screens. Let us say the average medium-sized home has twenty-four windows. This means that twenty-four screens must be removed and transported to some place of winter storage—a garage or a basement. Concomitantly, twenty-four sashes (which defy all logic by being simultaneously heavy and fragile) must be carried from their place of summer storage to their appropriate windows. Very, very, very few houses have windows of uniform size and shape. (This is because architects have a vested interest in divorce: a happily-married couple requires only one

FARMER'S MARKET

domicile; once separated, they need two and the architects have doubled their business.) One of the more maddening aspects of putting up storm windows is trying to sort them out by proper size for each opening. It is an historical fact that this cannot be done. Despite the most elaborate systems of marking or numbering, I have never been able to make them come out even. I wind up either with two left over or three short and there always is a long vertical window for which nothing can be found but a long horizontal storm sash.

But, let us assume that a beneficent diety smiles and permits an effortless distribution of storm windows to their proper stations. You think you got the problem licked? Hah! It is beyond all laws of chance that twenty-four windows should remain six months in storage unharmed. Inevitably, at least one of them will have become broken by a falling bicycle in the garage or by juvenile winter sports in the basement.

I made it through one summer with all my storm windows intact. I gleefully carried them out and leaned them against the house preparatory to hanging. The wind blew down two of them, breaking both.

So, one of the heady joys of hanging storm windows is a journey to the hardware store to buy a new pane of glass. Have you bought any glass lately? It is sold by the carat.

Then comes the task of replacing the broken pane. Of all home handyman jobs, none is more infuriating than reglazing a window. You must chip out the old, iron-hard putty, insert the new pane and then struggle with glaziers' points, those nasty little tin triangles that are stuck into the frame to hold the glass in place. With any luck, you will break the new pane during this phase of the operation. Then you must re-putty the sash. I would just as soon try to push a king cobra through a knothole as to try to make a limp, gucky roll of putty behave. Putty you are trying to

remove clings to the wood and glass like a barnacle; putty you are trying to apply won't stick to anything, but instead sags and slips and peels off in tired festoons.

Well, anyway, now you have all your storm windows repaired and in place. You think you got the job whipped now? Hah! You forgot to wash the windows, didn't you? The permanent windows have acquired a layer of summer scum; the storm windows still bear the accretion of winter scum you were too lazy to wash off when you removed them the previous spring.

Consider the arithmetic of the matter. You have twenty-four windows, right? You have two glass sashes for each window, right? Each of the sashes has two sides, right? You therefore have 96 surfaces to wash and polish, a figure so close to one hundred as to make no difference.

Here comes the hopelessly insoluble dilemma of storm windows. Autumn in the Upper Midwest is irrefutably the most beautiful season of the year. Indian summer is a glorious elegy to high summer, a time of clear, brilliant sunlight and a faint, smoky haze upon the horizon. The warmth of the days is more precious because of the hint of frost that manifests itself at eventide. Poets depair of painting in words the flaming loveliness of autumn leaves — and I am no poet. Our senses quicken and our tissues are invigorated as the organism prepares itself for the heralded rigors of winter. We emerge from summer sloth to meet the challenge and relish the sheer zest of being alive.

I pray you tell me: what man possessed of any feeling at all would squander such a day —possibly the last—on the dismal drudgery of hanging storm windows. Wives nag. Wives threaten. Wives implore. Wives sulk. But, the man of sensibility sits and glories in autumnal wealth, unmoved by mundane calls upon his attention. Storm windows can wait.

They do—right up to the first hard freeze.

STORM WINDOW

Quite obviously, you can't wash windows when the temperature is twenty-eight degrees. You don't. At best, you huff around with red nose and chapped hands hanging semi-opaque storm windows over semi-translucent permanent windows. For years, my family has been unable to see out of doors from October through April—but what the hell is there to see anyway?

After receiving numerous complaints on this subject I finally found the answer. I increased visibility by reducing the number of layers of grime through which it is necessary to look. In other words, I have stopped hanging storm windows.

My winter heating bill is ruinous, but I believe in supporting local business enterprise. Minnegasco loves me. And, my soul is not only pure—it is serene.

SPRING LAKE, BIRD SANCTUARY

379   'fresh up'   WHERE THERE'S ACTION...   404

MINNESOTA VIKINGS

NOVEMBER EVENING

*A*AS A NON-NATIVE, my qualifications for talking on and on about Minneapolis perhaps are questionable. However, in one area I feel that experience makes me competent: I have had a reasonably complete sampling of the residential variety available in Minneapolis. My family and I have lived in the near suburbs, in the exurban countryside and in Minneapolis proper, on the very edge of downtown. This succession of abodes seems sufficiently representative to offer as a cross-section survey of the city's neighborhoods.

Our first home was in Crystal Village, a northern Minneapolis suburb about eight miles from the center of the city. It was typical of any postwar suburb. In 1940, it had a farm-rural population of 2,373. By 1950, it had more than doubled to 5,713 (to which the Morrisons contributed four more when they arrived in 1951). By 1960, it had more than quadrupled to 24,283 (minus six Morrisons who had moved two years previous).

This kind of growth clearly implies what Crystal was: a tract-builders' festival. We bought a home in a subdivision of 200-plus identical small houses with three bedrooms (each more miniscule than the 12-by-16 living room). Bulldozers had skinned the cornfields

MOUNT CURVE HOUSE

down to subsoil and extirpated all but the very largest trees.

The houses were the "little boxes" of the satirical song. Variations from house to house was skin deep. There was mathematically precise alternation — peaked roof, hip roof, peaked roof, hip roof, et seq. Minor embellishments around the front stoop and a bland spectrum of different colors also helped you find your own house.

It sounds ghastly, but it really wasn't. Agreeing that this is not the most felicitous or soul-satisfying way for human beings to live together, you nonetheless would have to be the most arrantly unrealistic esthete to insist that it is anywhere near being the worst. We bought our little house because it was one we could afford. Being freshly come from a brownstone semi-slum on Manhattan, we were grateful to have it. If it was modest, it also was new, neat and snug and it served our needs.

Besides, the neighborhood was not so terrible. The lots were large, the streets were curved and the terrain was irregular. In the landscant east, such developments pack houses into straight ranks like tombstones. Here was more openness, less rigidity.

Most of our neighbors were younger families like ourselves, settling into their first homes. The houses began to acquire individual personalities as their owners covered bald clay with sod, dug flower beds, planted trees, repainted in colors of their own choice and began tinkering with the cookie-cutter sameness of facade. Since they owned their houses, they remade them to suit personal tastes. No less than 92.6 per cent of Crystal villagers own their homes—a typical figure for the Minneapolis suburbs, which have about 88 per cent home ownership. The national average is 61.9 per cent.

Typically for a postwar suburb, ours fairly crawled with small children. They played and squabbled and rambled the nearby woods and

SUBURB

fields together. In due course, they trooped off together to the brand-new school only three blocks away. They grew up healthy and (for all I know) happy. Our neighbors were lower middle class wage-earners (the present median family income in Crystal is $7,100). They were the first Midwesterners we lived among. We found them friendly, open people —in strong contrast to the withdrawn New Yorker. But they did not thrust their friendliness upon us. It was an agreeable balance. We were happy in our Crystal house for seven years. But, we outgrew it.

The alternatives were to find another suburban house, move into town or go farther out into the country.

The suburban scene had begun to pall somewhat, but also, after New York, city-dwelling held little appeal. We made our decision almost by chance when on a Sunday drive, we happened upon a beautiful (and inexpensive) lakeshore lot at the farthermost edge of Eden Prairie township on the westernmost boundary of Hennepin county. The lake is a clear, deep sapphire gem — inelegantly named Lake Riley — set amid high, tree-covered banks. The area is agricultural, with but a handful of commuting townies living among the farmers. There were only two homes on our side of the lake and perhaps 15 more on the other side.

We were so smitten by the setting that we bought the half-acre lot the same day we found it, saved our money for almost two years and finally built a house.

We could hardly have changed our way of

life more radically. It was almost 25 miles to my office; the nearest store was three miles away in Shakopee; the kids had to travel more than four miles by school bus to the small, but modern Eden Prairie school; we had no municipal services; RFD mail; no city phone. All our immediate neighbors could quite comfortably sit down in our living room and did (sit down, that is—I hope they were comfortable). But, we found what we wanted: a setting of serene beauty. I could spend a Saturday afternoon lounging on the shore of "my" lake and store up enough easeful calm to last me through the most hectic work week following.

In spring, summer and fall, the country life was a joy. Winters, needless to say, were quite a bit less than that. Worst of all was total subservience to the automobile. With no public transportation available, either your car moved or you didn't. In recollection, it seems to me that my car didn't move very often.

We lived down a hill. I had a 200-foot precipitous driveway—more of a goat track, really. Every evening there was the agonizing hour of decision: Should you leave the car at the top of the hill or put it in the garage under the house? It was a poignant point. If you brought it down the hill and it snowed overnight, you couldn't get back up the hill the next morning. On the other hand, if you left it at the top of the hill, the weather might turn very cold and it wouldn't start. Of course, I usually guessed wrong.

Despite such meteorological harrassments, it was with a profound stab of regret that we finally decided to give up our lake. It was the commuting that compelled the change.

The squirrely working hours that are the lot of a newspaperman—and especially a saloon columnist—made the 50-mile daily round trip increasingly burdensome. For my wife to join me in any nocturnal activities involved complex logistical problems that would bug a

DOWNTOWN

D-day planner. Should I drive an additional 50 miles to pick her up, or should she drive in herself—leaving us with two cars in town —or should we use an intricate ploy that entailed a Greyhound bus ride from Shakopee? Also, as one with a congenital and paranoid hatred for automobiles, I was just plain fed up with driving so far, so long and so often.

As summer waxes fat and lazy, I still yearn for the pleasures and beauties of rural, lakeside living, but I am now a confirmed city man—so long as the city is Minneapolis.

My family—an unruly mob of seven people, two cats, a pet skunk, one newt and (until a recent series of disasters) two iguanas, an alligator and two guinea pigs presently dwells in a big, goofy 1900-vintage house that tolerantly accepts us all and provides ample room for us to get away from each other when intrafamilial frictions arise.

The neighborhood is quiet, congenial, graced with fine old trees and charmingly eccentric old homes and is peopled by a pleasant admixture of younger couples with numerous children, older couples now alone, almost every vocational and economic status—all creeds and colors, unsegregated and unconforming, living side by side and happily.

I am five minutes from work. A city bus runs past my corner. I can laugh at the weather and treat my formerly tyrannical car with silent contempt.

Every mode of living that we have experienced in Minneapolis has had its advantages and disadvantages. Each has been quite different from the others. This, I daresay, could be true of any city. But, I can personally affirm that Minneapolis has used me well, that the pleasures and satisfactions so far have outweighed any problems or frustrations. And, more important, there always has been a stimulating range of choice when we decide to change our way of life.

PARK AVENUE

SOUTHEAST MINNEAPOLIS

LA SALLE AND GROVELAND

CEDAR LAKE, FRANK LLOYD WRIGHT DESIGN

LAKE MINNETONKA RESIDENCE

GREEK ORTHODOX CHURCH, LAKE CALHOUN

SINCE 1834, when Gideon and Samuel Pond founded an Indian mission on the shores of Lake Calhoun, Minneapolis truly has become a city of churches.

There are some 450 places of worship in Minneapolis proper and more than a thousand in the metropolitan area. A rough count in a church directory (and an even rougher understanding of the finer doctrinal distinctions) indicates that about 30 religious denominations and more than a hundred sects are represented.

In addition to the major American denominations, the waves of immigration that built the city brought with them numerous national churches from Ukrainian Orthodox to Finnish Lutheran. In the last century, services in many of these churches were conducted in the language of national origin and provided a transitional period for new arrivals in a

CHURCHES

strange land. As the need diminished, most churches gradually adopted English language worship.

The present number and diversity of congregations in Minneapolis forbids either generalizations or detailed discussion. Another glance at the directory suggests that the religious population is roughly divided four ways among Catholic, Lutheran, the other major American Protestant bodies and finally the remaining smaller denominations and sects.

Minneapolis is the home of the nation's largest Lutheran congregation, Mount Olivet church, and also of such obscure congregations as the Eleventh Hour Trumpeters.

You cannot go many blocks on any Minneapolis street without passing a church. In architecture, they range from the massive solidity of the Basilica of St. Mary to the modern lacy, glass-and-steel beauty of St. Peter Lutheran on France Avenue at Fifty-Fourth Street.

Each is a facet of the history and of the people of the city—all, taken together, are a major feature of the Face of Minneapolis.

EASTER SUNDAY, BASILICA

MISSION CHURCH NATIONAL MEETING

CHRIST LUTHERAN CHURCH

PLYMOUTH AVENUE SYNAGOGUE

CIVIL RIGHTS RALLY

TYRONE GUTHRIE THEATRE

IN THE AUTUMN SEASON of 1965 (October through December), a calendar of theatrical events published in the Minneapolis Sunday Tribune listed no less than 252 performances of 49 different plays or musical comedies by 23 theater organizations in the Twin Cities area.

These totals do not include a large number of minor, special-interest or one-shot productions during that period and the calendar doubtless has other gaps due to lack of notice, oversight or unconfirmed schedules of reporting theater groups

Figures are difficult to come by because there is little conformity in classification of professional, civic, community and amateur stage companies around the nation, but more than local pride sustains the guess that the Minneapolis metropolitan area has more organized, active, permanent, regularly-producing theater groups than any other city in its population range.

It goes without saying that there could not be so vigorous a production program if there were not a large and enthusiastic audience to support it at the box office.

Grassroots theater is a phenomenon to be observed all over the country. It can be explained several ways—primarily perhaps by a television-induced hunger for a live and life-sized drama among an increasingly sophisticated and well-educated citizenry. The economics of postwar Broadway, resulting in more and more "safe" formula plays and splashy musicals with surefire starring personalities, also may contribute — assuming that more and more creative theater people despair of New York as a theatrical mecca. Stage experiments are coming to have a larger chance for hearing on this side of the Hudson River.

It is less easy to explain why there should be so healthy a taste for live theater in the Minneapolis area.

Northern Europe has a strong theatrical tradition and that part of the world contributed predominantly to Minnesota immigration. That could be one reason. Possibly our long winters generate a greater desire for dramatic diversion. No one can say with certainty, but it is plain that a taste for the stage exists here and that it is remarkably well satisfied.

It is good theater. A professional critic goes to a community theater production prepared to make certain allowances and discounts. Aware that such groups lack many professional resources of money, training and talent, he is not going to insist on rigid professional standards of quality. Such critics, and I am one of them, increasingly are pleased to find that these hard-working, imaginative people have earned the right to be judged sternly.

It no longer is a case of enthusiasts assembling in a church basement to cobble together a production of "Pirates of Penzance" or "Charlie's Aunt." Professional directors now are the rule, rather than the exception. Design, and technical and musical direction also are being drawn from fulltime practitioners. The people who show up for casting calls may be doctors or salesmen or office workers or housewives, but most of them have been active in the theater for years and have an impressive list of past credits in eminently respectable productions. Many have backgrounds of intensive stage training as professionals or theater students.

The mix does not always come out right. Sometimes a community group goes on with the wrong play or too meager a ration of talent and the amateur production is painfully so. However, as a personal estimate, I would judge the local work I have seen over the past five years to be at least 70 per cent worth seeing and more than 50 per cent of very real merit. I would even grade about 20 per cent of the shows as being virtually irreproachable—indeed, many of these provided me with a caliber of dramatic excitement and interest not regularly encountered in an earlier five years of attending Broadway theater.

This again raises the question whether an existing local taste for good theater has encouraged the creation of same or whether the prevalence of good theater has converted more and more people to the pleasures of theater-going. In either case, we are fortunate now in having both in abundance.

A faithful conservator of that taste and a worthy supplier to it for decades has been the University Theater, the practical working body of the University of Minnesota's speech and drama department. Ranking with the foremost university theaters of the nation, Minnesota's players have provided not only the best of theatrical fare to its numerous patrons but also a large roster of well-trained actors and other theatrical specialists to off-campus stages. Many have gone on to Broad-

way and to professional careers elsewhere. Many more have remained on home ground, the bulk of them pursuing other careers but retaining their love for and skills in stage work —which they contribute as part-time members of the local theater scene.

The University Theater for years has been the chief source for classical and traditional drama, but it also is a showcase for works otherwise unlikely to be seen here, those of the *avant garde* and experimental sort. The more formal productions are to be seen in Scott Hall, an outgrown and overworked little theater on the campus. In addition, there is a full annual schedule of "workshop" productions of original plays (many of them locally and student-written) in the Shevlin Hall Arena theater. The University Showboat, a converted stern-wheeler, has created a tradition of summer fun since its inaugural productions for the Minnesota Centennial in 1958.

It is almost redundant to speak of the Tyrone Guthrie Theatre, the resoundingly successful repertory theater founded in Minneapolis four seasons ago by one of the world's most highly-regarded directors and a self-proclaimed fugitive from the sterility of Broadway.

Since 1962, when he announced that Minneapolis had been chosen over four other midwestern cities as the site of his experiment in bringing top-level classic theater to the grassroots, there have been oceans of print on the project, its progress, its artistic and financial well-being.

National interest in the enterprise is attested by the presence of leading critics from New York and other major cities at Guthrie openings. Local interest has been even more intense.

It is my feeling that this latter is of a special quality. Almost any city will rally around and support a big-name attraction, whether it be a big league baseball team or a symphony orchestra. So indeed did Minneapolis

rally around Dr. Guthrie's first tender of a new and important theater for the city. A construction and maintenance fund of several million dollars promptly was raised by foundations, business corporations and private donors.

However, it was my own impression at the time that the interest in this enterprise transcended mere local boosterism or civic *noblesse oblige*. There was a real excitement, as though this theater was wanted for itself, not just as a prestige item. And I feel that a broad cross-section of the people wanted it— a sense that seems to me borne out by the audiences seen on any given night at the Guthrie Theatre.

The upper-class aura has not attached itself to this endeavor as it has to some other cultural institutions. "Society" may turn out in evening dress for the opening of each season, but street clothes are the real uniform of Guthrie patrons and the enthusiasm of all classes is unmistakeable. The classic theater comes alive here and speaks to all. It has become "our" theater and any community pride in it runs second to the personal pleasure its productions afford us.

The experience of Guthrie actors, drawn from all over and including the most respected theatrical personalities further bears out this impression. They have been cheerfully adopted by the town, have settled down in our residential neighborhoods and some at least have told me that they have come to feel like native Minneapolitans.

The oldest still-operating professional theater company in the area is the Old Log, which is located on the verge of Lake Minnetonka and for almost 20 years has been the region's principal summer stock company. The Old Log originally was old logs—a barnlike structure with plain wooden benches and summer-night temperatures and humidity that should have discouraged attendance but somehow never did.

A few years ago, director Don Stolz and his troupe moved into a beautiful new theater on the same grounds, heated and air-conditioned for year-round use and with an expanded production schedule. The main fare of the theater continues to be summery—farce and light comedy drawn from the successful Broadway hits. It has built a clientele that delights in such frolicsome efforts, but once or twice each season a serious play is presented that demonstrates the company's considerable dramatic ability.

Among the civic stage groups, Theater in the Round Players doubtless leads in status and seniority. It is the officially chartered civic theater for Minneapolis and it began in the auditorium of the YWCA. From the first, it attracted a dedicated body of actors and workers interested in serious theater. Among the pioneers in the "open" or arena staging, Theater in the Round Players evolved techniques of lighting and set design that now have been burnished to perfection. Parallel to this, it has built an acting company and a roster of professional and semi-pro directors that have created some of the most meaningful stage offerings in the city.

Attempts to balance the program have resulted in some minor comedy presentations that were less than successful: this is plainly an organization that is at home with worthier things. When they are at peak performance, they are truly magnificent, with no apologies asked or given for amateur status. A recent production of "Streetcar Named Desire" vied favorably in my mind with the Broadway original; an even more recent rendering of Eugene O'Neill's "A Touch of the Poet" was superb. No theater-lover deliberately skips a Theater in the Round Players production.

Given the taxing circumstances of civic theater operation, the suburban Bloomington Civic Theater is a fascinating case history. Of modest beginnings and ambitions, it started work in a Catholic church auditorium. In-creasingly successful, it raised its sights and startled everyone with the announcement that it was going to undertake "Guys and Dolls," a fairly elaborate musical. Head-shakers shook their heads over the preposterously lavish $5,000 budget. The show was a smash; skillfully mounted, well sung, acted and danced and it came out in the black.

Since then, the Bloomington group has blithely tackled just about every top musical of the past fifteen years and has emerged not only unscathed but triumphant over each. The range has extended from the deftly-handled 1920's period spoof of "The Boy Friend" to the exacting musical and choreographic demands of "West Side Story."

A newcomer to the dramatic scene is the Firehouse Theater, which remodeled an abandoned 1890s Minneapolis firehouse with the express intention of producing *avant garde,* experimental and "Absurd" drama in the contemporary vein. It has had a troubled existence in its two years of life, suffering both from artistic and financial insufficiency. However, it is a stubborn organism and has not flagged in its productive efforts. At this writing, chances are good for survival. A skilled, youthful acting company finally has been assembled; it resolutely persists in its policy of off-beat drama, and its following is growing steadily.

Another suburban stage enterprise deserving of special mention is the Community Theatre of St. Louis Park, which bats a good .500 and which is totally unafraid of challenging shows. Alternating serious straight drama, comedy and musicals, this group has racked up such resounding successes as "Most Happy Fellow," one of the best locally-produced musical shows in a decade and has a lengthy record of similar successes.

Spottier in performance, but trustworthy for at least one respectable good show per season are such suburban troupes as the Edina Morningside Civic Theater, the North Suburban

Community Theater, the Richfield Players and the Footlighters, who operate in the northern suburbs of Fridley and Columbia Heights.

Children's theater in Minneapolis had been confined to occasional holiday presentations by the above civic groups until the Moppet Players opened in the Seven Corners neighborhood near the University. They took over an old police station. It was intended as a children's playhouse for the whole community, but had an additional function of recruiting the youngsters living in its run-down area to creative, purposeful endeavors. After three seasons, the staff divided. The Moppet Players still exists, while a cadre from the organization was invited to move to the Minneapolis Institute of Arts to form a Children's Theater Company there. The first production of the latter group was offered this year.

It would be woefully unfair, although this is a Minneapolis book, to ignore the theatrical life in St. Paul. Minneapolis theater-lovers make no such distinction and neither do those of the sister city.

The major St. Paul company, which draws heavily for patronage from across the river, is Theatre St. Paul, recently moved into a spanking new and especially well-appointed arena theater in the newly-completed St. Paul Arts and Science Center. Directed by Rex Henriot, it has become an anchor-house for the whole metropolitan area.

Other viable and artistically well-founded stages in St. Paul include the Eastside Theater, which grew up from a student mellerdrama lark in a cafe to acquire its own home and take on serious drama. Macalester and Hamline colleges have noted drama departments. The latter recently was given the Edyth Bush Theater, formerly a privately-run, handsome theater founded by the ex-actress wife of a wealthy industrialist.

Mention is due, also, for the Twin Cities'

only regularly producing satirical revue, The Brave New Workshop. It was born in Dudley Riggs' Cafe Espresso coffee shop on East Hennepin. Written and acted by local newspapermen and college students, it has had its ups and downs as far as material and income go, but has gained an appreciable audience. This year, it has moved to a new location on Hennepin Avenue near Twenty-Sixth Street and is going strong.

CHARLIE'S CAFE EXCEPTIONALE

WALKER ART CENTER

MEL JASS

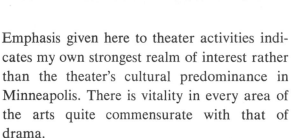

Emphasis given here to theater activities indicates my own strongest realm of interest rather than the theater's cultural predominance in Minneapolis. There is vitality in every area of the arts quite commensurate with that of drama.

However, as nationally-recognized institutions, there perhaps is less discussion needed about the Minneapolis Symphony Orchestra, for example, or the city's major museums—the Minneapolis Institute of Arts and Walker Art Center. They quite effectively carry their own identities and honors.

The Symphony particularly has had its impact on the nation at large and by its tours and recordings has made the name of Minneapolis familiar to hundreds of thousands. It is the most traveled major orchestra in the United States.

It was formally organized under its present name in 1903, when Minneapolis ranked 18th in population among American cities, but was one of only seven cities to have its own symphony orchestra (the second, incidentally, to be formed west of the Mississippi).

Audiences have kept pace with the orchestra's steady artistic growth under six successive conductors. Emil Oberhoffer was the founding spirit and leader for 18 years. Succeeding him were Henri Verbrugghen, Eugene Ormandy, Dimitri Mitropoulos, Antal Dorati and the incumbent director, Stanislaw Skrowaczewski. The orchestra presently offers about 110 concerts annually during its 30 week season and is heard by some 270,000 persons—including more than 50,000 school children at special Young People's Concerts. Subscription concerts fill the 4,800 seat Northrop Memorial auditorium to 92 per cent of capacity. In common with all other major symphony orchestras, the Minneapolis organization cannot survive on ticket sales alone. More than a third of a million dollars each year is donated by local firms, foundations and individuals to meet the inevitable deficits incurred by an orchestra dedicated to the greatest quality and quantity of performances.

Separate from, but adjunctive to the Symphony is the University's department of concerts and lectures, which regularly books in the world's leading soloists, singers, touring orchestras, ballet companies and a wide spectrum of foreign and native offerings ranging from a Chinese children's opera to the Moscow Symphony.

Professional opera in Minneapolis is almost solely dependent upon the annual visits of the Metropolitan's touring company. Invariably, these performances are sold out within a week after the engagement date is announced and a month or more before the Met sets up on the Northrop stage.

In recent years, much excitement has been generated and satisfied by the new Center Opera Company, which mounts smaller works —primarily contemporary—on the stage of the Tyrone Guthrie Theatre under the auspices of the Walker Art Center. With professional direction and (mostly) professional singers recruited locally, the Center Opera has made a large splash with many of its productions, notably "The Wise Woman and the King," which attracted national attention.

Another excellent musical group is the Minneapolis Civic Orchestra, composed mostly of dedicated amateurs, which presents concerts during the year. Conductor of this group is Thomas Nee, whose musical stature is as large as his physical stature is diminutive. Nee also is a moving spirit behind imaginative and delightful avant garde events combining music, dance, and film.

Dance is not an orphan art in Minneapolis, but it certainly is not the best-fed. Major visiting dance groups (Britain's Royal Ballet, the Danish Royal Ballet, New York's City Center) do sell-out business. The Merce Cunningham dancers and other contemporary groups attract wide interest. But, indigenous companies are few and small—reflecting the problems of this most severe and disciplined art which required lengthy training to produce good performers and whose good performances are in great demand elsewhere.

Local terpsers who need not apologize over-much for the above knotty equation include the Andahazy Ballet Borealis, a teaching-performing institution with annual full-dress productions, the Dance Guild Theatre, the Contemporary Dance Playhouse, the Dancer's Forum and two University groups, Orchesis and the Robert Moulton Dance Theatre. These groups help satisfy the demands of dance-buffs.

The plastic arts are most healthily served in Minneapolis. The Minneapolis Institute and Walker Art Center have earned national respect not only for the quality of their permanent collections, but for the vigor and calibre of the exhibitions they have organized for extensive tours.

Although smaller, Walker is the senior museum, at least if you recognize its origins. T. B. Walker was a pioneer lumberman who devoted a good portion of his wealth to collecting art. With increasing taste, he bought European art, classic pieces and antiquities for his private collection. It was typical of Walker (who was instrumental in making the exclusive Athenaeum into a public library) that his private collection by 1879 was accessible to the public and ultimately, with the building of the Walker Gallery in 1927, became a wholly public treasure.

Reorganized in 1940 as Walker Art Center, this museum has become a contemporary and "swinging" repository of modern art. Old T. B. might (or might not) cringe at some of the far-out exhibitions that now are staple fare at Walker, but surely would applaud the museum's philosophy which is to make art not only available to all but as inviting, exciting, lively and as much a part of Everyman's life as possible.

Summer jazz concerts and Fourth of July picnics have been part of the fun; lectures and comprehensive art shows have been part of the seriousness. An avoidance of the solemn and forbidding is a ruling principle. Walker is one of the few museums I know that permits gallery-visitors to smoke. It gives parties on the slightest pretext—and the bottles are not confined to Cezanne still-lifes.

Walker lives up to its "art center" concept by sponsoring every kind of artistic expression from music to dance to film to theater (including its contributing partnership with the Guthrie Theatre) to industrial design and crafts to nutty and only semi-serious "happenings."

It houses an "anchor" collection of representative traditional art from the 16th through the 19th century (plus one of the world's finest collections of oriental jade and ceramics), but Walker's prime strength is in 20th century painting and sculpture, of which it owns excellent examples of all the major artists and art movements right up to the emerging present. Of tremendous value in a time of rapidly evolving new art are the exhibitions of foreign painting Walker has assembled and imported to Minneapolis. The "London Scene" show and a recent Argentine show provided rich and startling glimpses of artistic ferment around the world.

The Minneapolis Institute of Arts, which celebrated its 50th anniversary in 1965, is more staid and seemingly better fits the popular notion of an art museum. Until a few years ago, in fact, there was a pronounced stuffiness about the Institute. Its Graeco-Roman facade was a suitable front for the classic works that dreamed upon its walls.

However, this permanent collection is acknowledged to be one of the finest in the country. Being irreplaceable, great art is priceless—but the collection has a book value of more than 25 million dollars.

The Institute was the doing of a group of wealthy civic and business leaders belonging to the Minneapolis Society of Fine Arts, who determined on building a dignified home in place of its then makeshift exhibition space. With the donation of land by Clinton Morrison (alas, no relation) and a half-million dollars in pledges, the massive structure became a reality and opened in 1915. It has been a going operation since.

The thing is that now it is going more than ever. Although there has evolved a tacit sharing of functions whereby Walker is the primary showcase of contemporary art and the Institute (because of its magnificent classical collections) remains more firmly rooted in the past, the stuffiness has departed. It is perhaps too much to ask that the Institute should swing, but in its matronly way, it has been shaking a lively leg. Modern art is warmly welcomed—including a recent large show of the wildest Pop art.

Some years ago, the galleries were rearranged so that a museum-goer can literally walk through time, make a chronological progress in art history from Egyptian times through succeeding periods to contemporary artists. Along the way are momentous milestones—Rembrandt, Titian, El Greco, Delacroix, Corot, Matisse, Degas, Van Gogh. Each is represented by major works.

Of special interest is the American wing, which surveys the finest of native painting. The Institute's oriental collections, those of antique silver and period furniture and of primitive and pre-Columbian art are other troves of beauty.

The museum legally and literally belongs to the people of the city and they seem to know it. More than 200,000 visit it every year—a figure equal to about half the population of Minneapolis. Its annual budget tops a million dollars.

There is much talk these days of a "cultural explosion," which is a somewhat dubious figure of speech. In Minneapolis, there has been a history of interest in and appreciation of all the arts from the city's beginning. This has grown steadily with the city (and with the whole nation, for that matter). What we see is not a sudden "explosion" but a product of slow growth that has reached a magnitude so impressive that we, ourselves, are surprised by it.

REMBRANDT'S LUCRETIA, MINNEAPOLIS INSTITUTE OF ART

WHEN IT COMES TO NIGHT LIFE, Minneapolis
is hardly Sodom and Gommorah or, for that
matter, either half of those twin cities. On
the other hand, neither is it a town with
nocturnally retractable sidewalks.

Minneapolis swings. It just has a somewhat
shorter rope than New York, San Francisco
or Chicago.

We partake, in our pleasures and entertain-
ments, of Midwestern conservatism. This,
however, is not as stolid as it sounds and it
wears a cheerful face. Put it this way: sin is
not a lucrative commodity in Minneapolis,
but fun and good living are. On a given Friday
or Saturday night, things are as lively as one
could wish and there is an impressive variety
of alternatives available to the fun-seeker.

Literally dozens of superb restaurants—in my
estimation more than in any other American
city of our size—vie with each other in excellence of food and gracious opulence of
atmosphere.

Drinking spots with one or another form of
live entertainment abound and are crowded
every night from Wednesday through Saturday. The sheer volume of traffic indicates that
Minneapolitans enjoy going out at night and
that their tastes in amusement are catholic.

The most visible center of this activity is
Hennepin Avenue, upon or immediately
abutting which are all the downtown movie
houses, all the gaudier nightclubs and strip-
joints and most of the late-hour eating places.
Like such streets everywhere, Hennepin has
a garish look at night and a tawdry one by
day. Neon blares in a cacaphony of color.
There are penny arcades, jewelry stores spec-
ializing in cut-rate engagement rings; sou-
venir shops, paperback book stores, army
surplus stores, a few pool halls. There is the
false, fluorescent hospitality of short-order
eateries, the trumpery flash of movie mar-
quees and sad, empty doorways leading to
upstairs dance studios, health parlors, beauty

STRIPPER, HENNEPIN AVENUE

154

DAYTON'S WINDOW

colleges, small fleabag hotels or dusty offices of obscure businesses.

Here, too, you find the sin—or the pallid prurience that passes for sin in most of America. Bright-lit entrances lead to smoky, raucous bars that feature 85 cent highballs in tiny glasses and a steady parade of girls on the back-bar platforms who remove their clothing with a languid boredom.

The customers are much more interesting to watch than the similacrum of sexuality taking place on the tiny stages. They share an aura of combined loneliness and longing — both quite unlikely of assuagement on that night or in that place.

There may be a few sportive young bucks—many perhaps come straight from the nearby Greyhound bus depot and an expectant journey to the big city from some small Minnesota or Dakota town—but most of the strip-joint patrons are older men. They are bored salesmen killing an evening, womenless men of every description, others who (for whatever reason) don't want to go home, and a leaven of elderly men who doubtless are there more in search of enlivened male camaraderie than to watch the girls. They all have the wistful air of men who yearn otherwise, but who know that the strident gaiety, fellowship and flaunted eroticism are synthetic.

These restless seekers do not make up the bulk of those thronging Hennepin at night. There are couples and parties simply enjoying the action, perhaps slumming for the fun of it. There are the younger boys and girls, some on dates, but mostly in groups of their own kind, who are taking in a movie, having a hamburger or a milk shake or simply drifting about for the sake of being where the lights and crowds are. There are movie-going couples and families.

And, your Hennepin crowds are by no means the bulk of those on any given night who are going out in Minneapolis.

The better restaurants are more or less evenly divided between downtown and the suburbs. So are the supper clubs and entertainment spots.

As mentioned, Minneapolis feeds its people well. Visitors from the largest cities are uniformly surprised at the number and quality of first-rate restaurants that exist and prosper here. National gourmet groups and magazines as well as numerous publications devoted to travel and the good life have singled out the city itself and numerous of its eating places for special praise.

Many of our restaurants enjoy the status of institutions—Charlie's, Harry's, Schiek's—because of their long years of continued excellence. Since the war, scores of other top-drawer dining spots have come into being and many established places have refurbished their decor and menus to meet the prevailing high standards.

Significantly, new restaurants in Minneapolis start out on the top rung. They must, in order to attract patrons with so many others to choose from. Typical is the brand-new Northstar Center, which planned a first-class restaurant, the Rosewood Room, into its complex of hotel, office and 'shopping space. Within two years, this restaurant had received one of the grudgingly-granted Holiday magazine awards.

Some years ago, a medium-sized, older hotel, the Dyckman, installed a French restaurant with a highly-trained European kitchen and staff—and promptly became a headquarters for Minneapolis members of all the gourmet societies.

There has been a countrywide decline in hotel food, but when the Sheraton chain opened its new hotel here, not one but two quality restaurants were included in the plan. It is obvious that Minneapolis not only expects, it demands, good food, gracious surroundings and special service when it dines out—which is frequently.

Suburban restaurants, most of them of postwar vintage, are no less responsive to this tradition. A new motel in Hopkins — the Hopkins House—included a lushly decorated restaurant with a continental menu almost as a matter of course. The White House in Golden Valley serves its area (and the rest of the city) with impeccably prepared and presented food, including an elaborate Cantonese menu. After a fire, a St. Louis Park bowling alley with an attached cafe rebuilt itself. The cafe turned into a charmingly designed restaurant, the King's Inn, with excellent food. A new restaurant in the southern suburbs opened on an almost overwhemingly lavish scale: the Camelot is not only vast, but fairly reeks of expensive quasi-Arthurian decor. It has been packed since it opened its doors.

The list could go on and on, but the point is plain without belaboring it. This plentitude of good eating, moreover, is relatively reasonable in price. Compared to the better restaurants in our largest cities, good food here is not expensive. The average meal in the best restaurants is between three and five dollars.

One final gastronomic observation involves a paradox: although the largest ethnic groups in Minneapolis are Scandinavian and German, there is not one major restaurant serving exclusively or even predominantly Scandinavian or German food. There are Mexican, Chinese, Lebanese, French, Italian, Japanese, English and Polish restaurants. You can even get a first-rate Indian curry. But nowhere will you find a commercial eating place that offers an authentic smorgasbord or a full German menu.

Eating, of course, is only part of a city's night life. The night club scene is another part. The pattern of night club entertainment in Minneapolis parallels that of other cities and currently (maybe permanently) has joined the others in a slump.

The economics of the entertainment business have changed profoundly in the past fifteen years. "Name" entertainers long ago priced themselves out of the general market—primarily because of the voracious demands and high salaries of television, plus the equally insatiable entertainment requirements and open-handed liberality of that weird Never-Never Land, Las Vegas. Except under special circumstances a club owner in a medium-sized city cannot afford to book a top performing star—or he does so in the dead certainty of never recovering his nut.

Through the 50's here, more than a dozen spots offered top-list entertainment—singers, musicians, comedians, personalities and speciality acts—most on a year 'round booking schedule. The inflation of entertainment costs gradually pinched out the name policy in most of the places, which came to rely on small house bands or trios, featured local vocalists—or in some cases piano bar entertainment and various fad attractions such as Twist shows or, at this writing, the Go-Go plague. The last top-star club in Minneapolis was Freddie's, which at one time was booking in the likes of Ella Fitzgerald, Mort Sahl, Shelley Berman, Erroll Garner, Oscar Peterson and George Shearing—at prices up to $8,500 a week. Freddie's went broke, as have many star-policy clubs across the country.

Most of the jazz establishments have suffered similarly: top musicians also command heavy fees. Herb's Bar, one of the best jazz spots in town, fell victim to such economics—and to an urban renewal project that razed the building. Some of the former jazz places on Hennepin now have only strippers. Big Al's, which has housed Ramsey Lewis, Ahmad Jamal and their ilk, now can afford but rare bookings of such pedigree. Davy Jones' Locker, which has a lively continuing entertainment policy, likewise brings in a big name only at infrequent intervals. The suburban White House presently is virtually alone in booking nationally-recognized acts (primarily high-class jazz), although it, too, is financially debarred from the biggest names.

Meanwhile, more modest, but still superior music and song go on in night spots. The youthful Edgewater Eight has earned respect in only a few years for its zestful, professional singing and dancing at the Edgewater Inn. Schiek's Sextet, which pioneered this kind of presentation, is as much an institution as the venerable restaurant at which it appears. Jazz is primarily generated by local groups—young musicians of skill and imagination who merit the attention of knowledgable devotees of new music forms. All of the better supper clubs and restaurants have live music, most of them with bands for dancing.

Minneapolis is a one o'clock town. State law forbids the sale of liquor after that hour (or on Sunday). Stepping out does not include all-night jollity as it might for revelers of requisite endurance in New York or Chicago. This imposes its own tempo on Minneapolis night life. After one a.m., the downtown empties and the neon starts winking out.

However, there remains a small but colorful segment of the populace that becomes visible after the bottles are corked. These are the night people, most of whom are employed in the night spots—and some of whom simply emerge from wherever they stay before midnight. The best observation posts are such establishments as the Market Barbecue, which stay open most of the night (without liquor, of course) and which don't do much business until the others have stopped doing it.

Bartenders, waitresses, musicians, entertainers (frequently including well known visiting names) off-duty policemen, civilian swingers who aren't yet ready to go home, newspapermen just finishing their tricks, any or all are likely to drop in for food, coffee and conversation. On upper Nicollet, the Chestnut Tree has a similar clientele, laced more strongly with the younger set—and often wrestlers finishing up a night of grunt-and-groan at the Auditorium. Giovanni's on Hennepin attracts a rather more raffish element from the strip-joints.

It is safe to say that no one has ever been killed by the frenzied pace of night life in Minneapolis, but by the same token, there is not much likelihood that anyone will die of boredom. Barring King Farouk, there is a bit of something here for everyone.

Except on Sunday. That, swingers, you can forget!

ST. ANTHONY FALLS, FLOOD TIDE

RIVERS HAVE A SPECIAL BEAUTY. Unlike placid lakes, rivers move. They have a life and—more engagingly, they have a destination. Rivers go somewhere and when you stand on their banks, your imagination goes with them. Oceans are vast things of awesome beauty, but rivers have manageable dimensions: you can see across them and fit yourself into their perspective. Rivers are friendly ribbons of beauty lacing the land.

All this being true, it is a sad irony that whenever a river passes through a sizable community, it is ravished of its charm. The river almost always is the reason for the city's existence. It is an economic asset that has turned a one-time hamlet into a teeming place of business. And, of course, in exploiting the river, the city-dwellers destroy the beauty of their stream.

It has been thus in Minneapolis. The town was founded and has prospered because of the Mississippi River—or more precisely, because of St. Anthony falls, which provided waterpower for the pioneer lumber and flour mills.

Paintings and sketches from the 1840's show the falls as a plunging cataract of wild majesty flowing between and around craggy, tree-clad rocks. A couple of decades later, photographs record a dreary, jackstraw complex of lumber mills lining the banks on both sides, smothering the setting of the falls in industrial ugliness. And soon the falls themselves were completely tamed: excavation of waterpower tunnels so undermined the ledge of the falls that it began to disintegrate and an artificial apron was built across the river, imposing geometrical orderliness on what had been natural, tumbling beauty.

The lumber mills now are gone and only a few of the huge flour mills that grew up with them remain along the river banks in the vicinity of the falls. Yet, the legacy of commercial drabness still clings to the river at this point and upstream all the way to the northern city limits.

Very few of the industrial installations now on the river have any relation to its economic value. Water power has become relatively unimportant and river transportation is utilized by a minor proportion of the businesses along the watercourse.

The controversial Upper Harbor project, a series of locks and dams to permit barge traffic above the falls, has been substantially completed and its promoters insist that the commercial usefulness of the upper river will be greatly enhanced.

However, most of the factories, warehouses, and other business structures now in the area are there simply because it has always been an industrial district. It looks like one.

Many of the buildings date from before the turn of the century and are built of the heavy, laminar native limestone. Streets often are still cobbled and many are narrow and steep as they drop down to the river's edge. A shabby gloom pervades the blocks of blank-faced, tight-packed buildings, with their streaked walls, littered loading docks and small, dirty windows.

Except along Hennepin Avenue, where it spans the river across Nicollet Island, there are virtually no residential structures near the river nor even small corner groceries and bars that would bespeak any ongoing neighborhood life. This is a place to which workmen come by day and leave at night.

As a reporter, I have had opportunity to visit the riverfront industrial area at night. A warehouse fire, perhaps, or a body found in the spillway gates of a power plant, or some violent transaction beween the derelicts who sleep in boxcars and various hidey-holes under bridges and wharfs.

Although I had in the past been taken by literary accounts of the romantically sinister Thameside district of London or the Seine waterfront in Paris, I was unable to work up a single delicious shiver amid the squat, scowling buildings along the Mississippi. Even the thought of an armed footpad lurking in the shadows of these ill-lit streets would have been more comforting than such bleak impersonality.

It is just plain depressing—the more so, I felt, when once, at 3:00 a.m., I had to walk five blocks to find a tiny warehouse office, feebly lighted and containing a nightwatchman who let me use his telephone after a drunk had driven his car over a retaining wall and into the river.

There still are remnants of the old walls, dams, spillways and channels that harnessed the river's flow—plus the works of a still-

NICOLLET ISLAND, SPRING FLOOD

existing water power installation on the west shore. On the opposite bank, the Main Street Hydro plant of the Northern States Power Company has similar, now uneconomic, works.

Standing on a crumbling basin wall, you get a feeling of the river's strength that is made more spooky by its silence. The water does not roar or splash or plunge. The surface moves with a slow, mighty roiling as it is drawn off somewhere underneath and carried through conduits to drive a wheel or to be discharged at some point downstream. The monster has been leashed, but all its sullen force remains.

Out in the river, the water slips silently and smoothly over the curved surface of the apron that once was a cataract. Only in spring-time high water do you hear the boom and drone of an angry river—and even that is muted.

Amid all of this man-made lifelessness, the bridges are a relief to the eye. The famous Stone Arch bridge, built in the 1880s to carry Great Northern trains across the river and still in use, is a solid, sensible structure, but its very utilitarianism gives it the sturdy grace of a Roman aqueduct. The Hennepin and Third Avenue bridges are not objects of beauty in themselves, yet seen from the river level, the high leap of the one and the sinuous curve of the other—as well as the bustle of traffic on both—enliven the scene.

Below the falls, the river makes a sharp right-hand bend at the University of Minnesota. This is the limit of the industrial ugliness. Below that point, the river moves through a deep gorge of especial beauty. If we deplore what happened to the upper river (even as we acknowledge its economic inevitability) we can be immensely grateful to the foresight of early park commissioners who systematically acquired for public use all the land along both banks of the lower river to its confluence with the Minnesota.

They bequeathed today's city some seven miles of continuous park overlooking the river, with winding drives, footpaths atop and below the bluffs and picnic and parking areas.

The future of the upstream portions remains uncertain. With the best will in the world, the transformation of established commercial districts is never easy and frequently is unfeasible. However, both Pittsburgh and St. Louis have pointed the way in reclaiming their urban river frontage as an esthetic asset to the community.

Minneapolis' Lower Loop redevelopment project has eliminated many blocks of scabrous blight riverward from the immediate downtown area. Some day, as now is being planned, the river may rejoin the town—but many difficulties, including the intervening presence of two major railroad rights of way, must first be solved.

GRAIN ELEVATOR, STONE ARCH BRIDGE

*Y*OU DO NOT CUSTOMARILY find a legacy of a city's commercial history in saloons—although they are interesting places to go looking for it.

Today's Minneapolis is a center of elite, sophisticated industry, including electronics and space technology, yet the locations of liquor establishments are a direct consequence of its earliest big industry.

No, the sale of booze was not the boom business. It was lumbering. The 1847 sawmill at St. Anthony Falls cut only 15,000 board feet of lumber per day. By 1900, a sprawling complex of mills along the river banks was turning out 474,000,000 feet daily.

The logs to feed all these voracious saws were floated downriver. With them, of course, came the loggers. It is a fair conjecture that when the loggers reached Minneapolis, they had worked up a thirst.

Back when Minneapolis had board sidewalks, a special problem confronted the city fathers. The heavy iron-caulked boots of this robust army of loggers chewed the sidewalk planks to splinters and necessitated constant maintenance work. The solution that suggested itself was to confine the loggers—and therefore the damage—to as small an area as possible. The easiest way to do that was to restrict the distribution of saloons.

The result was the so-called "patrol limits," a kind of *cordon sanitaire* beyond which no establishment could dispense strong waters. Needless to say, the "patrol" refers to police patrols—roistering loggers also could do considerable damage to citizens and to each other as well as to sidewalks. But, the initial impetus for the boundaries was solicitude for municipal property.

Today, the patrol limits still exist. They have been modified somewhat. A gerrymandered enclave extends southward to the area of Twenty-Sixth Avenue and Twenty-Sixth Street —formerly the "Hub of Hell" where the big

BOARD MEETING, HONEYWELL

railroad shops were located and where, apparently, mighty thirsts also were generated. A few special liquor licenses have been issued to establishments outside the patrol limits. However, the overwhelming bulk of Minneapolis bars—whether posh cocktail lounges or workingmen's saloons — are situated downtown north of Franklin Avenue, in northeast Minneapolis and in the northern part of the city near the river.

The steady depletion of forests within a feasible distance to the city doomed the lumbering industry and the last big mill was dismantled in 1921.

This decline in no way doomed Minneapolis, which from the first enjoyed an expanding and — more important — a diversified economy. Timber was but one of the natural riches in the huge region to which the city was both gateway, commercial headquarters and transportation center. There was iron ore to the north. There were endless acres of wheat to the west. There was water power—the life pulse of Minneapolis right up to the point in history where its size, commercial importance and skilled work force had attracted so many other industrial and financial interests that the city was viable with or without the plunging waters of the Mississippi at St. Anthony Falls.

Before that point, lumbering and flour milling were the twin industrial giants. Flour milling

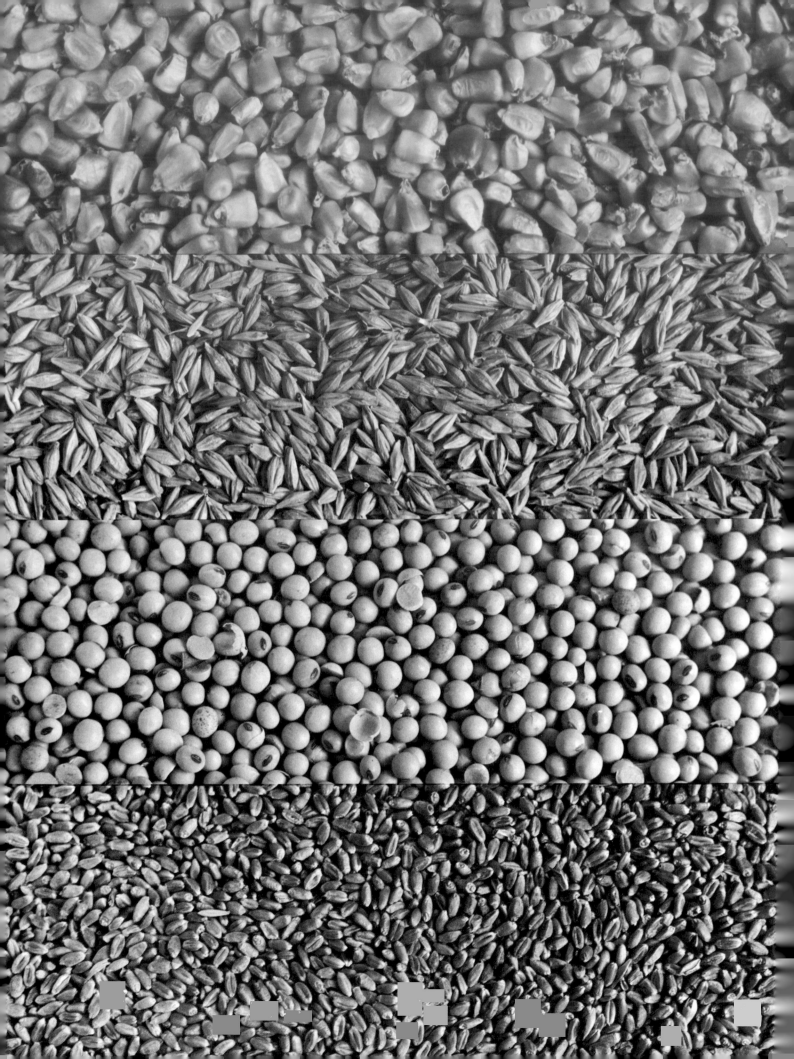

GRAIN EXCHANGE

THE PIT

MUNSINGWEAR

FASHION SHOW

not only has survived the sawmills but remains today as a major source of wealth.

The genesis of the flour industry was the government mill built in 1823 (at the foot of what is now Seventh Avenue South) to serve the Fort Snelling garrison. It had a "single run of buhrs"—millers' jargon for a set of grinding stones to convert the hard grains of wheat into soft flour. This old mill, enlarged and modified from time to time, operated for an amazing 56 years—until it was torn down to make way for another, bigger flour mill in 1879. It did not stand alone during this time, of course.

A private grist mill was built on the St. Anthony river bank in 1851 and in 1853 Ard Godfrey built his historic mill on Minnehaha creek. The first big commercial installation was the Minnesota Mill on Hennepin Island, with five run of stone, built in 1854. It cost $16,000 and made $24,000 profit in its first year of operation—a clear portent of the industry's future greatness. The first mill devoted solely to flour manufacture on the west side of the river was the Cataract Mill, built in 1859. Four more mills, each larger and more modern, went into operation during the 1860s.

So the history goes. So were born the names that increasingly moved into the nation's kitchens literally as household words: names such as Washburn, Pillsbury—and Crocker. George W. Crocker, of Rowlandson & Crocker, was partner in the 1865 Arctic Mill and "Crocker's Best" was an eminently successful brand for years. His fictional descendant, the agelessly handsome matron known as Betty Crocker now affords spiritual and material succor to millions of brides across the land.

The lore of milling is specialized and perhaps out of place here, but at least one development is vitally significant to Minneapolis. Spring wheat used to be considered an inferior grain for milling, its flour selling for one dollar a barrel less than the product from winter wheat. But, a Civil War hero, Cadwallader C. Washburn, and his partner, George H. Christian, listened to a French miller named Edmund LaCroix and in 1870 patented a process based on a technique whereby nutritious but formerly wasted portions of the wheat kernel (known as "middlings") could be detached from the hulls, reground and added to the flour. Almost overnight, the superior "patent flour" made from spring wheat commanded three dollars a barrel more than the formerly preferred winter wheat product. Mill efficiency also increased from 25 to 90%. The implications of this, not only to Minneapolis millers but to the farmers of the northern Great Plains where spring wheat flourished, are almost incalculable.

In 1866, eight mills at St. Anthony falls produced 172,000 barrels of flour. The following year, 13 mills ground 220,000 barrels. By 1876, the million-barrel mark was reached and four years later, that figure had doubled. One year after *that,* production was up to 3,142,000—and doubled again in the next five years. The ten million-barrel mark was reached in 1895 and the peak of 18,541,650 came in 1916. Subsequently, there was a relative decline from first place as Buffalo, New York, overtook Minneapolis as first milling city in the nation, advantaged by preferential rail rates that made it more economical to ship bulk wheat via the Great Lakes and distribute Buffalo's finished flour to the huge population centers of the east— or overseas.

Nonetheless, Minneapolis continues to rank second among the great milling capitals of the nation and is headquarters for the five largest grain millers in the United States. A series of consolidations beginning in the 1880's has led to the present Pillsbury Mills, General Mills, International Milling and other recognized corporate giants.

Almost every city's history records a major

disaster and that of Minneapolis took place in the milling district.

At 7:10 p.m. on May 2, 1878, the roof of the great Washburn "A" mill rose 500 feet in the air with a stupendous explosion that splintered windows and knocked down pedestrians as far south as Nicollet Avenue and Third Street. The immense mill structure disintegrated and the blast shattered adjacent mills, causing two more mighty explosions that demolished the Diamond and Humboldt flour mills, three smaller mills and a sash factory and machine shop, as well as extensively damaging three large flour mills across a canal from the site of the explosions.

Heavy timbers, stone, iron beams and human bodies were hurled over several acres by the blast. Fires completed the work of destruction and spread to other buildings causing heavy damage to three other large mills.

Eighteen men were killed instantly. The toll would have been much heavier but for the hour—the large day shifts in the mills having left work. Wild rumors of dynamite blasts prevailed pending the true explanation: super-fine flour dust suspended in the atmosphere of the mills ignited like gasoline vapor and the blast raised more dust to spread the explosion to other nearby mills.

The fragments of bodies recovered from the ruins were buried in a mass grave at Lakewood cemetery, where a monument was erected by the city's milling interests. A stone plaque memorializes the tragedy at the larger, more modern Washburn "A" mill that was erected the following year on the site of the old and which still stands today.

As lumbering and milling rose to their dominant position in the city's economy, other industries grew up on a lesser but proportionate scale. Earlier, it was iron works, farm machinery, railway equipment, paper, woolen weaving and knitting, food and feed processing, garments, furniture, and similar manufactures having a ready and growing market in a region booming with new settlers. Minneapolis was the manufacturing center, St. Paul the principal commercial city in the state. Over the decades, this distinction has become less meaningful, but the two municipalities — only ten miles apart — maintain quite separate identities. One sound explanation for this is the pattern of railroad development, an enormously significant factor in the growth and importance of the cities. Because of the terrain of the Minnesota and Mississippi river valleys, St. Paul is easily accessible by rail from the south and Minneapolis only from the west.

Quite naturally, the former city grew up as a jobber and wholesaler for goods manufactured elsewhere, while the latter could receive and process agricultural products from the western plains. Both cities, therefore, became railroad centers. And, since the only convenient river crossing once was at Nicollet Island, railroads "passing through" had to maintain facilities in both Minneapolis and St. Paul instead of concentrating in either and, perhaps, bringing about so complete a merger of economic interest that a political union might have followed.

To speak concisely of the business scene in present-day Minneapolis is to discourse in statistics. Together with St. Paul, it is the largest market area between Chicago and the West Coast and is the nation's seventh largest distribution center.

Hennepin county has 1,729 manufacturing establishments and, unlike the past, no one or two industries dominate overwhelmingly. In 1964, the area's two largest firms employed only 4% of the total work force and the top 85 hired only 30 per cent.

As of 1963, 1,730 wholesale businesses had total sales of just under 4 billion dollars; 3,974 retail stores rang cash registers to the tune of 860 million. Bank clearings in 1965 exceeded 30 billion dollars.

In 1965, total non-agricultural employment

was 649,538, of which 173,530 were in manufacturing at an average weekly wage of $119. Fifty-seven Minneapolis area firms employ 500 or more persons. The new world of technological industry is well represented and growing. In 1955, 26,000 persons were employed in electronic and related science industries; eight years later, the number had almost doubled to 48,600—and one locally-born computer firm, Control Data, grew from scratch to 6,000 employees in only six years. A sketchy profile of Minneapolis manufacturing is seen in the major employment groupings: machinery (non-electric), 17.2 per cent of total non-agricultural employment; instruments and related products, 16 per cent; food and kindred products, 12.7 per cent; metal fabrication, 8.1 per cent; printing and publishing, 6.7 per cent; electrical machinery, 5.2 per cent; apparel, 3.9 per cent; paper, 3 per cent.

According to a 1960 National Science Foundation study, the Twin Cities area had 2,387 scientists. So far, they have not done much damage to the sidewalks.

FLOUR EXCHANGE BUILDING

LINDAHL OLDS

GRAIN WORKER

PILLAR OF GRAIN EXCHANGE

*T*HE FIRST EDUCATIONAL INSTITUTION in Minneapolis was the Indian school and mission built by the Pond brothers in 1834. The first school for white children was opened in a frame shanty in 1849 on the St. Anthony side of the river—Miss Electa Backus, teacher. The following year, two school districts were organized.

And the year after that the University of Minnesota came into being. Education always has and still does march smartly in Minneapolis. Quite obviously, however, the early beginnings were modest. These first schools had but a handful of pupils. The fledgling University was really a preparatory school and consisted of a two-story wooden building.

Its first teacher was the Rev. Elijah W. Merrill, who came to Minnesota in the understanding that he would receive a fixed annual salary. He was quickly disabused: he was intended to eke his living out of student fees, amounting to from four to five dollars per quarter apiece. In fact, he had to organize a series of lectures

NORTH HIGH

to help pay for the building he was to teach in. The lectures, at one dollar a head, reportedly bedazzled and bewildered most of the frontier audience.

The board of regents that had been charted by the territorial legislature to govern the affairs of the University set about to erect the first building of the college-level institution. It was an extravagant stone structure costing the shocking sum of $49,600—and it no sooner got under way than a series of natural and economic calamities began to plague the optimism of the founding fathers. The Rum River dried up and the University was unable to realize any return from sale of timber on its land grants. The Panic of 1857 shook the nation and $40,000 worth of university bonds went begging for many months until they finally were sold for $34,000.

Despite all this, the new building (later called Old Main) opened on May 28, 1858. New dissension arose over the intended exclusion of female students, but a lively press battle brought a reversal and the University of Minnesota coed was born.

Governor Ramsey trumpeted the state's advances: "Where in the world have 200,000 people accomplished so much as we have and that, too, upon a very small capital and at a rate of interest that would grind the very Alleghenies to powder . . . We have churches, schools, academies and colleges superior to any to be found in the whole extent of the frontier and the educational interests of our youth have, from the earliest days of our settlement, engaged the attention of our people."

It might be mentioned as a way of typifying the birth pangs of the university that Reverend E. D. Neill, the first chancellor, once threatened to resign because the school did not have enough money even to buy postage stamps.

This is not the place to rehearse the long and distinguished history of the University of Minnesota or trace the development of the city's public school system. However, one thing should be noted that makes Minnesota unique among most state universities: its charter predates the admission of the state to the union by seven years. Consequently, the board of regents enjoy an autonomy from the state legislature and have jealously exercised it. Although dependent in great part on the lawmakers for operating and capital funds, the academic and administrative affairs of the University are not subject to legislative direction.

Today, the University of Minnesota is one of the nation's largest—the fifth largest in fact. It would rank even higher but for the recent trend in such states as New York and California to lump many diversified schools and campuses together into a single "paper" university. Minnesota is spread over several facilities, also, but the overwhelming majority of students are on the Minneapolis and St. Paul campuses (34,574 out of the total enrollment of 39,634 in the 1966 winter quarter) and the Minneapolis campus far, far overshadows the Agricultural School in St. Paul.

The size of the student population on this single giant campus is a major problem particularly as enrollments continue to climb. The nine per cent increase from the 1965 to 1966 winter quarters is not unusual. One result of such growth is the expansion of the campus across the river to the west bank and the Seven Corners area. The influence of Gown on Town will certainly become even more pronounced as the University physically moves toward the fringes of the downtown district.

In addition to the University, of course, there are smaller private colleges in the Twin Cities, most of which are in St. Paul—Macalester and Hamline, for example—but the city line is of little consequence to the commuting Minneapolis student. Both cities make up an educational complex that is the center of the entire state's higher educational system.

Public school education, including Minneapolis proper and all the suburban and rural school districts of Hennepin county is of the impressive dimensions that would be expected in a large metropolitan area. The total enrollment for all grades in 1964-65 came to 190,826. This does not, of course, include enrollments in the many private, parochial and church-affiliated pre-college schools.

The Minneapolis area statistically is in the forefront of American education at all ages. Almost three-quarters of Hennepin county's 466,378 residents who now are 25 years of age or older went to high school and beyond. Of these, nearly one-quarter attended college and 53,277 (or 11.4 per cent of this age bracket) finished four or more years of college.

Minnesota, which ranks midway in population among all the states, is near the top of the pile in expenditures for education. Studies have indicated that Minnesota spends more per capita on education than any other state in the Union.

Just as did the first pioneers building a city in the wilderness, today's Minneapolitan wants schools for his children. The results of this long historical demand can be seen in the state's record of having the lowest illiteracy rates—and the nation's highest scores in army induction tests.

UNIVERSITY OF MINNESOTA

THE MALL, UNIVERSITY OF MINNESOTA

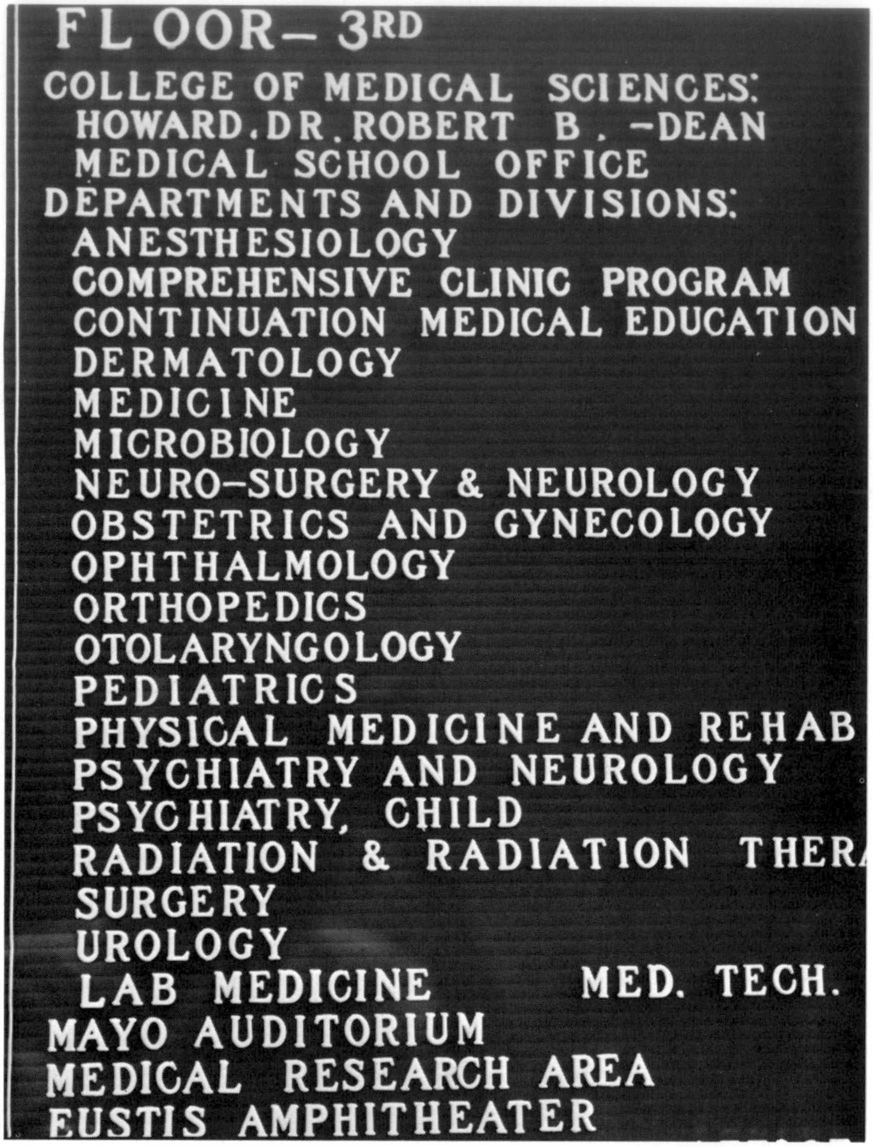

FLOOR— 3RD

COLLEGE OF MEDICAL SCIENCES:
  HOWARD, DR. ROBERT B. —DEAN
  MEDICAL SCHOOL OFFICE
DEPARTMENTS AND DIVISIONS:
  ANESTHESIOLOGY
  COMPREHENSIVE CLINIC PROGRAM
  CONTINUATION MEDICAL EDUCATION
  DERMATOLOGY
  MEDICINE
  MICROBIOLOGY
  NEURO–SURGERY & NEUROLOGY
  OBSTETRICS AND GYNECOLOGY
  OPHTHALMOLOGY
  ORTHOPEDICS
  OTOLARYNGOLOGY
  PEDIATRICS
  PHYSICAL MEDICINE AND REHAB
  PSYCHIATRY AND NEUROLOGY
  PSYCHIATRY, CHILD
  RADIATION & RADIATION THER/
  SURGERY
  UROLOGY
  LAB MEDICINE   MED. TECH.
MAYO AUDITORIUM
MEDICAL RESEARCH AREA
EUSTIS AMPHITHEATER

DIRECTORY, MEDICAL SCHOOL

CAP AND GOWN DAY

SCHOOL YARD

BETWEEN CLASSES

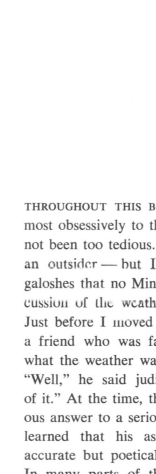

THROUGHOUT THIS BOOK, I have referred almost obsessively to the weather. I trust it has not been too tedious. Possibly it would be for an outsider — but I am willing to bet my galoshes that no Minneapolitan finds any discussion of the weather less than fascinating. Just before I moved to Minneapolis, I asked a friend who was familiar with the locality what the weather was like.

"Well," he said judiciously, "there is a lot of it." At the time, this struck me as a frivolous answer to a serious question. I since have learned that his assessment was not only accurate but poetically just.

In many parts of the country, you can go

whole weeks or even months without any weather. It may be warm or cool or clear or cloudy or dry or rainy, but it remains consistently so—and it is in perfect consonance with the season and the region. It is not "weather" in the sense that it is sufficiently good or bad to merit comment.

In 15 years of Minneapolis residence, I cannot recall more than three days hand-running that have been without "weather."

The weather in this part of the continent does not fool around. Whatever it is, it is with fervor and zeal and dedication. It does not bother merely with snowing if it can work up a good rousing blizzard. Why have a plain old shower when a cloudburst is so much more lively? A warming trend may not stop until it hits 104. A cold snap poses a real hazard to brass monkeys.

Not unsurprisingly, Minneapolitans talk more about their weather than they do about anything else—sports, neighbors, children, their jobs, the high cost of living or sex. This dominant topic of conversation is never dull because the weather never is. The chief difficulty is that the weather may change when you are in mid-sentence and your observation on it is obsolete before the words are out of your mouth.

All this makes the weather sound consistently bad—which is libelously far from the truth. The tendency toward extremes applies in the positive as well as the negative sense. If bad weather can be bad, good weather in Minneapolis can be incredibly fine. And it will seem even more so being sandwiched in between bouts of bad.

In earlier portions of this book, I have celebrated the beauties of spring, the gentle pleasures of summer, the tangy glory of fall in Minneapolis. Now we come to the orphaned stepchild of the seasons: Winter.

If you are expecting me to say something wholeheartedly nice about winter, you better go buy yourself someone else's book. Rather,

I would prefer to address myself to the question of why we put up with Minneapolis winters.

I am about to let you in on the best-kept secret of the age: Minneapolitans really like their winters.

I arrived a greenhorn in Minneapolis. It was gorgeous mid-May, but everyone I met took ghoulish delight in warning me of the horrors to come when winter returned. Although I discounted this as the customary hazing of a newcomer, I admit I felt qualms. Well, the subsequent winter was, as a matter of fact, fairly grisly. But that is not the point. What is the point is that by the next year I found myself—now a seasoned veteran—retailing wintry horror stories to the newest group of greenhorns.

This is the close-held secret. Minneapolitans think they hate winter and are vociferous in saying so. Only an outsider like myself can penetrate their unconscious fraud.

Some observers have put it down to a kind of mass masochism — perhaps the gloomy Nordic pessimism of an Ibsen or Strindberg. I disagree wholly.

What I perceive at work is a perverse pride. It is compounded of gratitude at having survived, an earned sense of courage and fortitude, plus an enriching fellowship forged out of commonly-shared rigors. It is rather like those secret cults and fraternities or the manhood rites of primitive tribes that subject their initiates to hardship and humiliation the better to awaken their sense of strengthful belonging.

For this ego-satisfying process to work, it is essential that the trials be harsh and severe. Moreover, it is essential that the accepted members boast of the pains and privations they have endured. One mild Minnesota winter would not necessarily destroy the socially-useful effects of this process. A decade of temperate weather would, however, utterly destroy our morale and reduce us to the flabby inconsequence of Miami or Los Angeles.

What saga ever emerged from Tahiti or the Bahamas? The Norse tradition of manly struggle found in Snorri Sturluson unquestionably found its roots in a bunch of Vikings sitting around the ale hall and bitching about how hard it was to get the reindeer started that morning. Beowulf did not wear Bermuda shorts and sunglasses.

You cannot tell me that the hazards of winter are not cherished by Minneapolitans—in precisely the same way that a combat veteran relishes the perils of the battle he has survived. He has fuel for a lifetime of yarn-spinning. No one asks to be bludgeoned over the head, but it makes a good story after it happens.

Minnesota's winters, with all their agonies and uncertainties, are a never-ending source of adventure and stimulation. Even as we curse them, we are paying tribute to the fact that they keep us from being bored.

I, for one, could never again live in a bland, equable, uneventful climate where fair day succeeds fair day in a plodding cycle of eudiometric tedium. It would be like having Christmas every day or Oysters Rockefeller at every meal.

I have come to see that our seasons—given winter at its hairiest worst—keep us alert and alive by their sheer theatricality. Our constant, nervous glances out the window to see what atrocity the weather has cooked up for us *now* serve to give us a sense and a feel for the natural world that is denied those living amid unchanging weather. We are made aware of rhythms larger than ourselves and certainly larger than the pallid routines of daily existence, of trudging off to earn our bread.

This, I firmly believe, makes for mental health, just as the challenging rigors of winter make us physically healthier because we physically respond to them.

We are, praise be, spared the commonplace.

SNOW FUN, LAKE CALHOUN

BUS STOP

EAST SIDE SHOPPING CENTER

SKATERS, RIVERSIDE PARK

WARMING HOUSE, LAKE OF THE ISLES

LAKE OF THE ISLES

SKATING CHAMPIONSHIPS, LAKE HARRIET

7TH AND NICOLLET, MONDAY NIGHT

ICE FISHING, CEDAR LAKE

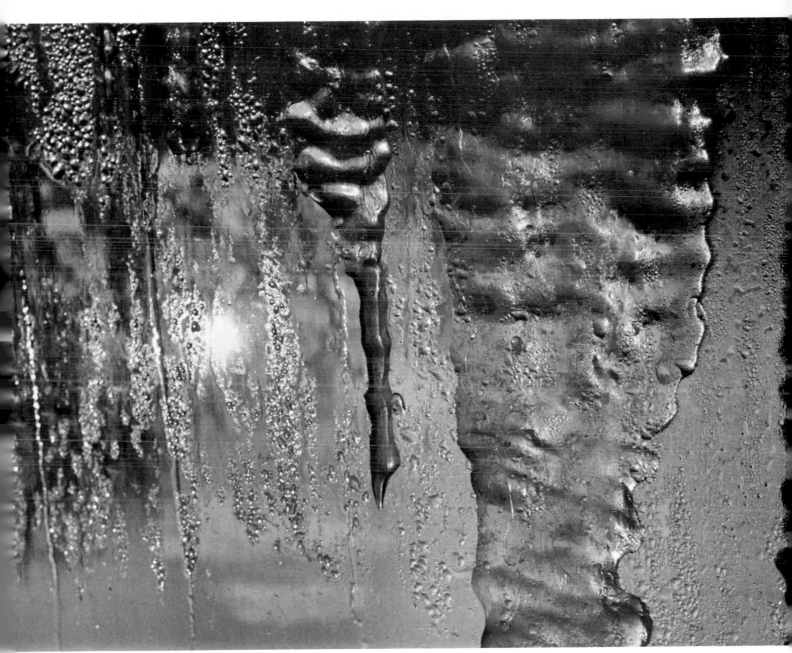

FROSTED PANE

Spring is an event in whatever part of the world that has winter. Consult any anthology of poetry.

But, spring in Minneapolis is more than just an event. It is an annual honeymoon. Usually it is delayed and the populace, after five-plus winterbound months is more impatient for the soft, warm, scented sweetness of spring than any repining bridegroom for his beloved. In our northern latitudes, spring is not merely the beginning of somewhat warmer days after a succession of somewhat colder ones. Spring is liberation. Spring is the opening of windows that seemingly have mouldered shut. Spring is shedding heavy garments, unwrapping scarves, taking off hats, unbuttoning jackets, casting overshoes to the farthermost corner of the hall closet.

Spring is freedom from the exactations of keeping warm— no longer does the furnace throb day and night in its relentless task of burning up your income.

Spring is freedom from snow-shovels, tire-chains, dead batteries, inhalers and lip-salve and the all-too-common cold. Spring is switching to gin and tonic.

Spring is a pale sun turned ruddy and gold. Spring is a keen, uncongenial wind turned into a gentle caress. It is grimly lifeless stone and brick and cement becoming warm to the touch, acquiring once more its own body

heat. Spring, for all these reasons, is splendid. But even more. Spring also is the time that Minneapolitans discover anew their city.

Every year, we sink down into the trough of winter. After the first pleasant snowfalls, that frost and frieze summer's familiar scenes with ornamental white, we lower our heads into our collars. We lower our eyes to the treacherous pavement. We seldom look beyond us farther than the nearest doorway offering shelter. The motorist's gaze is frozen upon the slippery street and is unseeing of aught to either side.

Ah, but in spring! There is the city again. Where has it been all this time? The bleak, black tree skeletons — from which we have averted our eyes because nothing looks colder than gaunt, bare branches — take on pale, pastel flesh that swells into rich, corpulent green.

Lawns—brown, then white, then dirty-white, then brown again — suddenly are cushiony, restful billiard cloth again. Roofs and building tops glow warm in the wakening sun after months of bleached winter light. Massed drifts of apple and plum and even spring flowers somehow seem superflous, almost gaudy, alongside the greater blessing of simple green and gold and the flesh-tone pink of the very air in spring.

Out of this new and miraculous underwriting of continued survival—no less miraculous because it checks in every twelvemonth—the city emerges. The eye freshens and sees it as if for the first time.

Minneapolis is a prettier city than most. The partisan might think it the prettiest. But, no popularity poll is needed in spring. In residential areas, its houses seem to breath well-being after months of pinched huddling against the winter. Its streets once more become arcades of sun-shot green shade. Its business districts, which frankly are no triumph of urban beauty at the best of times, look twice as good minus the curb-high slurry

ICE OUT

FIVE O'CLOCK

SAM MELE, MANAGER OF TWINS

of dirty slush. Its parks, lovely even in winter's worst, are even more lovely and inviting. Its lakes, freed of their icy, white winding-sheets, twinkle like the lively blue, seductively promising eyes of the prettiest fourth-generation Scandinavian girl in town.

Oh, yes, the girls. It is impossible to sort out the statistics, but I am convinced that one would find a higher percentage of fender-bender auto accidents in the first, flushed days of springtime warmth than in any other period of the year.

It is then that the girls emerge. They have been around all year. Despite their seeming absence, they do not migrate south. But, in winter, as do all of us, they retreat into cocoons of clothing. They become enshrouded in textiles, swaddled in heavy wool and fur. Outdoors, in winter, they hurry down the sidewalk, faces set against cold and turned from the wind, their forms and figures unknown beneath purdah-like pyramids of protective garment.

All at once, on a day in spring, these cocoons hatch. The girls are back again. They blossom in the warmth. They slough off the unseemly bulk of cold-weather gear and can be seen for what they are: girls. They no longer scurry down the sidewalk. They stroll. Their faces receive and reflect the sun. The breeze is an attentive gentleman, not a demeaning boor.

Heaven help the poor male driver on days like this. The distractions are inhumanly many. Every street corner, every 20 feet of thoroughfare provides distraction to the eye. Clutches and gaggles and coveys and bevies of pretty girls suddenly seem to spring out of the earth and command attention.

After the winter's long famine, here is a feast. In the face of such competition, the foolish doings of automotive traffic up ahead seems unworthy of notice.

For all of us, for child, youth, adult and oldster (sitting on his sun-warmed porch for the first time after an eternity of winter) spring is special. The only sweating we do in winter is sweating out spring.

226

MINNEHAHA CREEK

LORING PARK

MINIKAHDA CLUB

NORTHROP, OPERA AUDIENCE

Photographer's Note:

I would like to thank all the gracious people of Minneapolis who helped make the photographs possible by permitting me entry to their homes and places of business, and thanks as well to the people who were photographed without their knowledge.

The photographs were taken with both Rolleiflex and Hasselblad cameras and the film processed in Acufine developer.

Colophon

This book was printed at Meyers Printing Company in Minneapolis. The paper was made by the Northwest Paper Company of Cloquet, Minnesota. The body type is 11 point Times Roman. Reproduction is by offset lithography in a technique developed by Meyers Printing Company especially for this book.

... December AD 1858. before

... lly came before me Alfred E

... dmund Rice, Francis R.E.

... her husband) the owners and

... Rices addition to Minneapolis

... d by and for said owners. and

... me and title of Hancock: &

... their said attorney have signed

... me this December 14-1858.

..., Notary Public Hennepin County Minn

... und Rice, Francis RE Cornell.

... Julia L Hawley and her husband,

... d E Ames their attorney in fact:

... lition to Minneapolis as surveyed.

... nship 29 N Range 24 West of the 4th

... n and marked "Reserved" on the plat.

... ston, J H Andrews.

Office Register of Deeds }

Hennepin County Minn

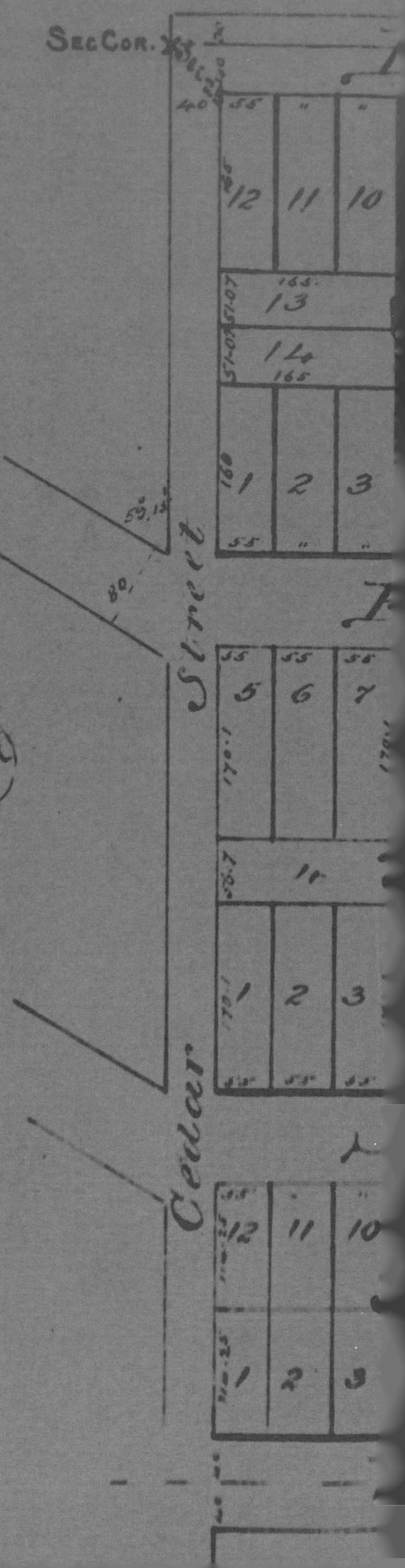